ALSO BY

CARLO LEVI

WORDS ARE STONES
1958

THE WATCH
1951

OF FEAR AND FREEDOM
1950

CHRIST STOPPED AT EBOLI
1947

(*THE LINDEN TREES*)

TRANSLATED FROM THE ITALIAN BY

Joseph M. Bernstein

ALFRED·A·KNOPF   NEW YORK

1962

THE

LINDEN

TREES

CARLO LEVI

L. C. catalog card number: 61–17910

THIS IS A BORZOI BOOK,

PUBLISHED BY ALFRED A. KNOPF, INC.

Published simultaneously in Canada
by McClelland & Stewart, Ltd.

FIRST AMERICAN EDITION

Originally published in Italian as
LA DOPPIA NOTTE DEI TIGLI.
Copyright © 1959 by Giulio Einaudi editore S.p.A.

Funkenblicke seh' ich sprühen
Durch der Linden Doppelnacht
GOETHE
Faust, Part II, Act V,
SCENE 3, LINES 21–2

THERE MAY BE a land where the roofs of ancient
houses still rise sharply, like the cottage of Baucis
and Philemon; where green branches are mirrored in the gently flowing streams. But in what
memory has their smoke been lost—and their
life? And with what ashes are their flowers
covered? Lynceus, on his tower, has sounded the
lament: fiery glances have flashed through the
double night of the linden trees; the true things
have died in frenzied suicide.

Now, in order not to see the inner desert,
another night lingers: the night of eyes shut
tight and hard-working hands; in which, with
reason and passion closed in sleep, even the
emptiness is divided.

$\left(\text{F O R E W O R D} \right)$

I HAVE returned to my house in Rome, in the midst of trees already in blossom and with bees humming around the medlar tree. It is year's end. The sky is so blue, the winter air so full of golden dust, that the eyes, accustomed to the muted colors of the North, seem dazzled by the splendor of a too joyful, almost unbearable intensity—like the eyes of some nocturnal bird which, surprised by the first rays of dawn, blink and look dazedly about for an old familiar wall.

If I propose to tell here of the simple things I happened to see in the course of an all too brief journey, it is not only in order to aid my memory and compare my impressions with those of my readers—

who, of course, are free to correct them where they seem wrong. Nor is it in response to the friendly insistence of my publisher. I would not presume to write a study on so vast a theme as Germany. How could I? I did not go there, like a hunter in the wilderness of facts, looking for incidents or news items or eyewitness reports; nor do I intend to venture beyond the limits of a modest true story of an ordinary, uneventful trip. But it seemed to me that, however sketchy and hurried my impressions may have been, I could not avoid expressing them; not because of their intrinsic importance, but because the country I have seen is, for all of us, even those who do not realize it, bound up in some way with a basic fact of our existence. I have just come back from Germany, jealous Germany—from its public squares filled with Christmas trees.

I had never been in Germany before. The bridges over the Rhine had remained a boundary I had never crossed. Only once, in a slight haze, did I glimpse the German plain, from the height of a Gothic spire in Alsace (where Church triumphant and blindfolded Synagogue, opposing goddesses of the imagination, merged in the roseate stone warmed by a still young and innocent sun). It was an August morning in 1939, when the whirlwind of destruction was about to begin. Then many years (many centuries!) later I flew over Germany, without seeing anything but the eternally fleecy clouds beneath which were hidden millions of Germans—their houses, forests, and industries, their emotions and problems, their bigness and power.

This omission, or gap, or lack of direct firsthand knowledge may seem strange. It seemed strange even to me. But you must remember that for many people Germany remained for a long time a forbidden land —even before the sealed trains and the one-way trips to the concentration camps. Visiting was prohibited by force of circumstance, by laws, and by arms; and perhaps too it was prohibited within us, by the sense of the sacred in a remote and obscure moment of conscience. But where are the prohibitions now? Everything is open. Time, like a raging flood, has swept away forlorn trees and ruins—as well as memories. So all we have to do is to look, if we want to see and understand. We can look with eyes and spirit divested of passion, even of the living residue of old passions and old questions; we can look as on a new thing.

Frequently, before my departure, I would ask myself: What am I going to see? A country without ancestors, born of the ashes, alien to the permanent themes of its history? Or do its past and present stand together, diverse elements intertwined yet separate? Which of the many Germanys of culture and history shall I encounter? How much of their residue or hybrid mixture will I find in the Germany of today? What is appearance and what reality in this heartland, so rich in fantasy and emotional associations, so well defined in our mind? What has happened, or what is happening there now, after all we have lived through?

"After Maidenek," the poet Umberto Saba used to say—and he meant after the horrible evils of Nazism—"all men have in some way been diminished. All of us—executioners and victims—are and for many more centuries to come will be much less than we were before." All of us . . . not only the Germans. As in a Chaplin film, executioners and victims alike, once they reach their outermost limit, have the same look and the same destiny in a world of upheaval. Yet even at the extreme edge of the dehumanized a new human moment can come to birth. What has remained beyond the human slaughter? What has been reborn after the mortal crisis which, for all of us, brought to the surface of reality the blindest, most hidden, and most outlandish atrocities? All of us were forced to feel these atrocities, to fight them, to re-examine the past embedded, like prehistoric fossils, within the deepest layers of our consciousness. Meanwhile, above this bedrock we slept soundly in our unawareness. We built cities and homes; we fostered civic and family pride; we devised myths of man, progress, and history—only to face once again, in modern and unpredictable forms, the same monsters so often slain by the heroes of mythology. And why was it in Germany that this cataclysm, this world-wide epidemic, broke out? Why did it find there its carriers and its symbolic protagonists?

The crisis, bursting forth with climactic violence before our eyes, had long revealed itself everywhere to a greater or lesser extent as it infiltrated the world like some hidden infection. It was the revelation—and the demonstration in deeds—of the break in man's unity. And leaving aside all the recent and less recent social, political, religious, and economic reasons for atrocities and total war, we see that Germany more than any other country, in the centuries of its storied history and the individual lives of its inhabitants, has borne within itself this permanent trait of disunity—as a danger, a tendency, a sense of mission. Set against this tendency to fragmentize, the unifying and "Olympian" harmony of Goethe stands out in massive relief, rising up in lone splendor like a mountain in the midst of a formless plain. Perhaps his solitude makes us feel at times that there is something unspontaneous in him, a shrillness and a smugness that come from a constant exercise of the will. Perhaps the Germans' incessant longing for the classical, the pagan, the ideal, for perfection in form, arose as compensation for their centrifugal nature; hence too their passionate and dreamy yearning for the sun, for countries of the South—lands where the orange trees bloom. Something has always been lacking in the German world in order for a complete and well-rounded adjustment to develop within the individual. This disharmony or disjointedness has produced, on the one hand, a distorted and isolated development of the emotions, as in expressionist or romantic sentimentalism, and, on the other, the crystal-like impassivity of pure reason and reasons of State. And it has carried to the extreme, as separate elements, all the problems and divisions, all the instincts and death wishes, all the institutions: army, rank, family; anarchic freedom as well as imperial rule; categories and universals—and, in the dense forest of these absolutes, dark anguish.

Since it is impossible to embrace the whole man, since therefore love—except for the fatal love of the

Tristan legend—and liberty are impossible, there remains only suicide as the equivalent of love. Suicide, in the form in which the whole society participates, implies the destruction of the world; or, reversing the picture, in its jealous prenatal form— unbounded freedom—it implies murder, the *Lager* or concentration camp, where *Arbeit macht frei*— where work makes one free. This monstrous inversion arises from a rent in infancy, from a blurred distinction between self and things that is prior to all history and individual development. If Germany is divided into two parts, it is because it is and has been everywhere divided, in its unconscious.

These matters concern all men. We can and must ponder them but not be judges of them. The very name of Germany is bound up with the most intense and irrational emotions: infinite hatred and love, boundless admiration and horror. Who, despite himself, does not recall—along with the sublime images and universal creations of German art philosophy, and technology—certain vivid occurrences at unique and crucial moments in his life? For us Italians, the tiny serpent's heads of the SS men of Vallucciole; the cold eyes of the Reichswehr soldier casually lifting the old man by the nape of the neck, like a dead cat, and then letting him fall dead on the ground; the fabulous monsters of expressionist art that became realities; the shaven heads, facial scars, thick necks, green-clad legs, and the sound of army boots by night on the pavements of Florence. . . . But this absurd violence—where was it? Was it only in them? Or was it, in some mysterious and necessary fashion, also in ourselves? Or was it a dream, the revelation of a time forgotten and covered over for thousands of years by the earth of the buried dead and then projected into reality, into that particular reality? To one who is not and can never again be either executioner or victim in spirit, whatever his status in the world, it takes more than meeting a Nazi on the street to make one hate his country in Nazi fashion.

The inner lack of unity is the condition which has made Germany the central figure of the universal crisis. But isn't it something even prior to this lack of unity: an absence of differentiation, an inability to differentiate? There can be unity only between distinct things. Some obscure portion of that world of forests and factories, of enormous and undefined power that seeks in vain to rush stubbornly into action, retains the old and basic characteristics of the primitive anarchic unity of the Germani who ate alone and built their huts in solitary isolation. It is the first stage of infancy, preceding any detachment, any freedom, any knowledge. Something remains of that primal period, something of the chaotic milk prior to weaning. The Nazi schizophrenia can only be conceived of as having been formed in that very first moment. Then came, as a necessary complement, Hitler's paranoia—to guide it and hold it together. That part of Germany which remains in the phase of prenatal humanity is not separated from things. It is not free; it cannot be loved and loving, but must devour and (never enough to satisfy its craving) be devoured. So we ask: When Nazism caused the Germans to discharge the horrible archaic content of their bowels, was it not perhaps because they had never been and could never feel sufficiently loved? Nests, feathers, the intimacy of walled cities, of homes and families, the most intimate, jealously guarded emotions, are not enough. (With the Germans can one ever believe in *dayenu*, the paschal rendering of grace?) These things are never enough if from the beginning a relationship of love and freedom, a differentiation from the mother, is missing. And what can be "enough"? Can an infinite number of relations suffice to fill this emptiness with love? Did a God never come? Or a man who would bring about union? This void, this inexpressible power, this unsatisfied longing, this need, must have been deep indeed if neither destruction nor blood rites nor magic and barbarous communions were able to fill it and appease it.

But the images that remain now, after the war, true or false, lived or seen or imagined in terror, are henceforth nothing but one of the moments in a past common to Germany and the world. At least we would like to think so. What impels us all is the feeling that the new can and must be different. Germany, perhaps more than any other country, is the place where we must look for it. Our very life depends on this new element. So does the future course of events, as well as the most insignificant thoughts and acts in our rebuilt homes. What is Germany today?

Before leaving I was curious to know what my very first impressions of that unknown land would be. For in all my travels it has almost always turned out that my feeling for a new country has been formed in an initial image, free of any bias or preconception, and not even influenced by any historical or literary background. This image—call it idea or intuition, vague sentiment or impression—becomes a kind of "crystallization," as in a love-at-first-sight experience. At bottom it does not matter whether this image in itself is accurate and basic: it is important that it be

alive and true. Then, like a key, it serves to open all
doors, explaining the multiple aspects of reality,
which in their turn alter it, or may even destroy and
eliminate it. This image may spring from a trifling
object—from a word, the color of the sky, the scent
of the air, from some comparison or contrast. It is
really an apprehension or perception of love: a
simultaneous awareness of oneness and otherness, a
very broad and vague synthesis of the consciousness,
powerful and revealing in its vagueness. The very
first moment I set foot on the sidewalks of New York
and Moscow, they spoke to me directly and forcefully.
What would Germany say to me on my arrival—if
only in the gesture of a passer-by, the sound of a
voice, a chance look?

This first image did not appear, or at least not
clearly enough to be discerned—perhaps because I
expected it. The one that did appear to me at the
outset was so literally similar to the one which,
despite myself, I had known and imagined, that it
was as if nonexistent. So I have had to seek and find
reality without proceeding from any initial image. If
the reader is willing to follow me through the pages of
this little book, he will go on an underground journey
with me, with twists and turns and without any pre-
conceived plan. For that is how the German reality of

today struck me: contradictory, ambivalent, and not easy to define. Judgment will therefore follow and not precede—and, wherever necessary, it will remain suspended. But if I may run somewhat ahead of my story, with its simple account of facts, persons, and ideas, I would say that this uncertainty of first impressions did not come from any special disposition on my part. It did not result from any lack of attention or clarity, but solely from the things themselves. Great minds of all periods, German and non-German, from Tacitus to Brecht, have spoken about Germany and vividly described it. Everything they have said and everything that has been said these past few years by the most varied and careful observers is, in some degree, true. A case can be made for praiseworthy and enthusiastic opinions; the same can be said for negative and critical comments. It seems to me that what the present-day onlooker sees is not a clear and distinct reality, nor does it manifest itself in a single clear-cut way. It is rather a reality that eludes one and remains concealed. Germany is hiding.

It does not hide from the visitor. On the contrary, it would be hard to find a people more open and confident, and apparently without any secrets, reticence, or shame. It does not hide its splendors and its wounds, its well-being, its reconstruction and recovery, its activity, its prosperity, its ruins, its feelings and problems and aspirations, its statistics, and its culture; it does not even hide its private life, its homes, families, foods, and habits. Nor does it hide its past, some aspects of which it might like to disavow. No, Germany is not hiding from others: it is hiding from itself.

Germany is still in shock. Perhaps, to be more concrete, I should say most of the Germans; or, according to my limited experience, those Germans, many or few in number, who define the general direction of the country, its dominant and collective feeling. Nazism and war were a trauma of immeasurable magnitude. Despite all appearances—peace, wealth, full employment, well-being, law and order, and even a certain humility (is it humility or humiliation?)— the trauma has not been overcome. It remains; it works in the depths. But by a natural process of repression, enabling the Germans to go on living, it is hidden. The time of horror and want, the collective sense of guilt, all the facts—the big and little and blood-curdling facts—that were called the "misery and terror of the Third Reich," now blotted out of memory, have not ceased to operate. It is precisely the mechanism of repression that makes them continue to operate at every moment in daily life. It seems to me that a deep inner censorship is at work throughout the entire country (in different and opposing, yet similar, ways in East as well as West Germany). I see it as a deep renunciation, voluntary or involuntary, conscious or unconscious; a constant self-mutilation. On the surface everything appears normal. In some areas, such as economic and industrial recovery, reconstruction, employment, the successes have been extraordinary. But what is missing in all these is the one value that can make them true, genuine, and complete. One feels the presence of something unfilled, a void, a forbidden point one is unable to approach. I am tempted to call it a neurotic disfigurement.

In every sense—geographically, historically, politically, and culturally—Germany has been the center of Europe. It still is. Its problems are our problems as well, and affect all of us. But it is an empty center: somewhat like the eye of a cyclone, the calm center in which the air is unnaturally still. All the Germans have gone to work. Their hard-working hands produce fabulous amounts of goods and wealth. The devastated cities have been rebuilt; cars speed over the finest highways in Europe; the houses are mirrored in the quiet waters of the rivers; the young people in love sit close to each other holding hands;

the forests breathe a sense of eternal peace. But it is
a wounded country, an offended country, offended by
itself as well as by others; a country with its eyes
shut, stubbornly shut. Beneath its mild and peaceful
and even harmonious exterior, it has perhaps never
been so divided internally—and not only by boundary
lines. Thus, creative originality, thought, art, even
politics, the dangerous and vital things, are, by an
instinctive need for survival, kept hidden. They are
left dormant, concealed, held in suspense. Germany is
sleeping, watched over by its instinctive censors and
by a curfew which has the illusory appearance of a
rebirth. No one today knows what is being prepared
in its millions of homes. Will it arise new and more
human? Will it awaken savagely? Or will it prolong
its sleep? At present Germany is still crippled, split,
rankling with guilt, speechless, tired.

Just as sick people take sleep or hibernation as a
cure, Germany is trying instinctively to get well by
refusing to face reality. Sunk in the dark sleep of its
forests, of its urban jungles with their factories,
cranes, wheelbarrows, cement bags, blast furnaces,
goods, money, and foodstuffs, it absorbs and digests
voraciously. In this sleep even dreams have been
repressed. Those who are awake and question themselves are few. For the moment, their thinking and

suffering do not count, except as poignant individual problems. They dream different dreams: new missions, new swords in hands that were better left open and empty. Foreign dragons—Fafnir and Fasolt—watch over this sleep. Once again that industrious society of dwarfs is tirelessly piling up a hoard of gold and burying it beneath the earth. Even in their mythology the capable Germans have foreseen everything! But are the foreign and domestic dragons really watching over Germany's voluntary and involuntary, magic and deliberate sleep? Are they presiding over its busy lethargy? Or, ignorant of mythology and history, are they seeking instead to awaken the sleeping country prematurely, to fill its void with arms and dreams of imperial greatness, to mend its division with army divisions? As so often in the past, the cry of *"Deutschland, erwache!"* is starting up again. And the danger is that, like a sleepwalker abruptly aroused, the sleeper will open its eyes with a mortal shriek of violent madness.

The German void is the darkness of sleep that frees one from the incessant and increasing waves of anguish. *"Oh, nun waren wir Nachtgeweihte!"* ("Oh, now let us be dedicated to night!") Germany's mythology and ritual magic put a cloak over its sleep. But what good are myths and magic, memories, images, and passions to one who wishes to see and lovingly embrace reality? Let us forget them. Let us leave them behind before we start out. At least let us act "as though" they did not exist. That is both right and necessary. Let us go to those swarming yet orderly cities, among the unknown yet familiar crowds, in a relaxed and open spirit, with our eyes of today. Let us simply tell about the little we happened to see and meet, without pretending to say any more than a few of the thousand things that can be discovered and told. Our bags are packed, the plane is on the field—let us take off.

$\left(\textit{THE LINDEN TREES}\right)$

(I)

O N C E again the Ciampino airfield appears before me, with its glaring lights in the early-evening dusk, and the vague shapes of planes outlined here and there like lonely birds. Then come the good-bys, the take-off toward an unknown place, other men, other lands, where everything is new and strange and different. And everything in us is new. Daily routines are suspended; the world built on habitual gestures and schedules is no more. Beyond the windows I can see the faint lights of Rocca di Papa shining over the hill of the Castelli. Everything is set: airline employees, porters, mechanics, baggage, and travelers— those uncertain beings, sitting with their newspapers in the waiting room, already tired of waiting.

3

Some American children are playing in the glass enclosure reserved for youngsters; it resembles a transparent cage. They may be leaving on a flight much longer than mine. Meanwhile they are twirling hula hoops around their bodies. How absorbed and serious they are, with their tiny turned-up noses and tufts of blond hair falling across their freckled faces! They are very good at the game, seeming not to move as the hoop twirls. Relaxed, natural, they behave as if born in the midst of a world like those hoops—speedy, fragile, and revolving. A little girl standing by and watching is given a hoop by her brother. Carefully she removes her wool cap and cumbersome overcoat and, stiffening her body, launches the hoop. But she is tiny and awkward; she soon tires of this monotonous and difficult twirling, which too often ends in her falling. Then she grasps the hoop, turning it vertically over her head and passing it under her lifted feet with perfect timing. She handles it like an ancient jump rope, one of those forgotten ropes of a childhood in a different age. She counts her jumps, stumbles, and finally gives the plaything back to her brother. Now the perfect and impassive circles begin again, an abstract endless revolving—like time, a clock, and countless destinies. The little girl directs (or thinks she directs) the spinning object with her

4

hand. The boy stands completely within a circle which, though prompted by an invisible movement on his part, envelops him and seems destined to continue forever—dominating him and setting him apart.

The green plastic hoop twirls . . . the propellers loudly twirl. Voices on the loudspeaker announce the departure. We take off, each for some personal and specific reason: a business deal, a meeting with friends, a conference; for study, pleasure, or necessity. We know where we are going. But do we know why we leave what remains behind and does not follow us? Perhaps travel is always a flight, an unconscious quest, an escape, an abandonment. So those who stay behind wave their handkerchiefs and their eyes fill with tears: they are the ones traveling backward in motionless time. Departures separate people. Sorrows and uncertainties, worries and decisions, repetition and monotony—all are left behind. But so is the delicious honey of happiness—the familiar steps, the usual sounds of an early-morning awakening, the clatter of spoons on dishes, a shout in the yard, the bird on the tree outside the window, the soft color of the sky. Thus soldiers leave for war in fear, humiliation, and sorrow, yet with hearts full of obscure joy at leaving their beloved wives and children, their regular jobs, their cherished yet hated routine of everyday living. And the words, the big words such as Native Land, Glory, Honor—and Death—are nothing but this longing to escape to adolescence, this desire to leave the real war of life to those others who stay behind. The plane engine, like a heart alternately contracting and dilating, expresses and bears within itself our contradictory feelings. It expresses our need for solitude, now and then, in the crowded world of men.

Perhaps each time I have left I too, like everyone else, have been impelled by some unconscious motive as well as by an obvious and practical reason. Yet I do not really think so. It is so hard for me to say good-by; it weighs so heavily upon me. Now, however, as I go to Germany for a lecture I could not get out of and to discuss things with some German publishers, I would say that nothing unknown or mysterious prompts me. I feel a kind of coldness and unaccustomed boredom. Everything seems familiar: the attendants on the plane ramp, the seat belts, the pleasant voice of the hostess, the caramel candies that go with our upward thrust toward the sky.

Inside the Lufthansa plane there is already an air of Christmas. As in some village chapel, the candles are lit among green holly wreaths that mask the

6

neon lights. For it is Christmas Eve, the gift-giving holiday of the northern countries; and tomorrow, Christmas Day, genial Santa Clauses with white beards and red costumes will appear on the public squares of Germany. Our flight through the darkness is so swift that it blots out all sense of transition. The lights below—streets, perhaps, and cities and landscapes of three countries without boundaries—are abstract and ceremonial symbols. The flight leaves us no time for the material changes in our bodies and feelings that occur when we proceed on slow overland journeys and make us similar to the places we pass through, as unwittingly we adapt ourselves to the changing languages, gestures, and aspects of nature. Nor does it allow for reflection, or the search for some order in the vagueness that lies ahead. With a start I realize that on leaving I have forgotten many things I thought I would need. This surprises me greatly, because it has rarely happened before. Yet I have left behind the German dictionary which was to supplement my meager knowledge of that language, a package of books about Germany, and a notebook with names and addresses. But what of it? The pleasant warmth and hum of the plane soothe me. I feel a vague sense of pity—for the Germans or myself? And now we are landing at the Munich airport.

The plane taxis across the field and stops in front of the ponderous Hapsburg façade of the waiting room.

The customs officials, too, resemble the architecture. As they examine the luggage efficiently and systematically, they look at you with indifferent eyes, not as a guilty party but merely as an object. There is something bureaucratic yet homey about them; some of the hardness and obsequiousness of an old and unforgotten imperial Austria. They are wooden yet paternalistic officials of a small country, narrow but knowing. The city is not far away. In the unexpectedly mild night air we pass a few suburbs cloaked in darkness, some well-planned avenues, and imperial statues gleaming white among the flower beds of the parks. Then, after we cross the bridge over the Isar, I see the façades of the 1900's on Maximilianstrasse, faithfully restored and symmetrically arranged on both sides. Only here and there, behind the monument to King Maximilian II, a dark patch or empty window still shows some signs of destruction. A few cars drive silently on the avenue. The people walking unhurriedly along the sidewalks, the little girls accompanied by their mothers, the blond little boys, the men warmly dressed and wrapped in scarfs, appear prosperous and secure. Behind their gestures one glimpses calm and orderly habits, a world in which

8

the narrow, finicky concerns of family and city may have the weight and certitude of the pyramids. At this evening hour, as all the inhabitants stroll leisurely to their evening meal, my first fleeting impression is of a peaceful provincial city, attractive, clean, rich, bourgeois, ensconced in the usual intimacies of family and profession—and in the boring mediocrity of well-being.

I enter the spacious and luxurious lobby of the Hotel Vierjahreszeiten—the Four Seasons Hotel. Barely twenty years ago four men with faces like death's heads sat here on armchairs and signed the Munich Pact, to the dismal relief of millions. And quickly all Europe bore the stamp of death. Now, on the same armchairs, jovial fat gentlemen are seated, smoking expensive fat cigars. Their wives, in evening dresses, gaze at them with admiration. A thin lady photographer is eagerly waiting for me at the entrance and introduces her daughter, an anemic little girl with a red overcoat and pigtails, who smiles and curtsies to me. That is the first part of the lady's assignment. Then she asks if she can accompany me to my room and take pictures of me with her flash-bulbs. She is an American woman from Berlin; after an autograph for the little girl and another curtsy, mother and child leave me. A veteran German journalist, with a big head and long hair, pleasant and perceptive in a solemn sort of way, is waiting to take me on a tour through the center of the city.

The streets of Munich remind me of Zurich. I see the same modern show windows, with the latest abstract designs by the decorators, and the same abundance of tobaccos, women's fashions, and exotic fruits. The pastry shops display wonderful Christmas treats: *Christollen* concealing their tasty richness beneath a thin icing of snow-white vanilla, and *Baumkuchen,* in the show window of Kreutzkamm's, the famous old pastry maker of Dresden, rising up like pylons over the surrounding plains—some covered with chocolate, some not. In the peaceful stillness of the broad, clean, half-deserted streets we stop at every step. The smallest shops are filled with almond-paste figurines supposed to bring good luck: bearded Santa Clauses, small boys astride a pig, and above all a rosy-colored baby, with a black top hat on its head, its diaper down, auspiciously and daintily engaged in eliminating a gold piece. This wealth, so innocent and so intestinal, blankets Germany.

The restaurant-beer hall on the square faces the pseudo-Gothic Town Hall with its ancient pillar and musical mechanical clock. It is crowded with customers, most of them in large noisy parties seated at

10

tables and waited on by waitresses in Bavarian peasant costume. They are good-natured people, simple,
prosperous-looking, resembling those you might
meet in some humdrum little town in Switzerland. If
anything, these are even milder and humbler-looking
and more unconcerned. But there is just a touch of
the "artistic" about them, a hint of "off-beatness" in
their conformism, which is in the city's tradition. Not
a trace, in these florid, smiling faces, of arrogance or
viciousness; rather a spineless softness, a blissful
expression of renunciation. Where, in these con-
tented faces of educated middle-class burghers, are
the monsters of painting and satire? As I continue to
observe them, I reflect: Perhaps if I look more closely
I shall see behind the mask. All that is needed is a tiny
shift, the slightest distortion of crayon or eye. Or
maybe, even in centuries gone by, that nondescript
expression, colorless and dull, and that air of pleasant
and unassuming familiarity were the reality. As if he
realized from my glances what was running through
my mind, a young Frenchman seated next to me
murmured: *"Il n'y a pas de monstres."* Then he
smiled as though he knew me and went on: "As you
watch them, they're the gentlest animals in the
world. What can lure them from their grassy meadows, impel them toward the most distant lands, drive

them to war, incite them to atrocities the greater and more senseless for being involuntary? It can only be some will outside themselves—the leader of the docile flock who does not know what force is driving him. What does a misled flock do? It can do all kinds of terrible things and end with a suicide leap over the cliff. . . . Yet, it is said, they are the gentlest sheep in the flock." He came to an end. Then, as the rest of the customers amiably watched him, he hunted vainly for his overcoat among the thick rows hanging from the clothes racks.

The same sort of people filled the cafés where, late that night, the journalist went with me in search of an Italian *espresso*. Stout men sat alone on benches next to fat little dogs wrapped in knitted wool sweaters and gazed at their pets with moist tender eyes. Young men languidly held hands with their girls; others, red-faced, drank thick soup or ate sausages. On the now deserted streets an occasional lone drunkard passed, staggering uncertainly from one side of the pavement to the other. My journalist friend was able to tell me, from each one's gait, whether his drunkenness came from beer or hard liquor. Christmas time in Munich is not the main season for drunkards; hence we could indulge in all sorts of subtleties as we analyzed the various categories of intoxication.

So we came to Cathedral Square. We looked up at the lofty towers on both sides of the façade, gleaming on high against the wintry sky. A night watchman wrapped in an old gray coat, holding a big bunch of keys, was making his rounds at all the gates. Hearing Italian spoken, he turned and addressed us: "I've seen cathedrals, many, many beautiful ones, when I was in Italy. I was there during the war. The one at Rovereto, Trento, Milan, the one at Orvieto . . ." He began to enumerate. He had been with the German Army all over Italy: at Cassino, Alatri, Anagni, Perugia, Arezzo, Florence, in the Apennines. "But the Italians," he asserted, "are hospitable." He was a Sudeten German, his face already old and with a large mustache—one of many who had not seen his native land again. He said he was sorry he couldn't speak Italian: "We learned Czech, then Polish, and then Russian. At that time we weren't so tired. But then we got tired. We were too tired to learn. We were even too tired to learn Italian." He gave us a military salute and went on his way. In front of those little houses asleep beneath sloping roofs, it seemed as though he were shouting the curfew call: *"Bewahrt das Feuer und auch das Licht Damit kein Unglück Euch geschicht! Lobet Gott den Herrn!"* ("Look to the fire and light, so no accidents will happen. Praise

God the Lord!") Light and fire—the dangerous life —are hidden in Germany's inner night, a stubborn and temporary night. *Lobet Gott den Herrn!* The night watchman's clumping footsteps died away in the darkness.

(1 1)

THE NEXT morning, under the pallid light of a winter sun filtering through very cold layers of gray mist and drifting fog, I found the same mélange of the banal and familiar and the grandiose and bizarre. Even after the greatest disasters and devastation, places retain, like a permanent portrait, the traits with which history has marked them. The city of Munich was celebrating its 800th anniversary. At that age, is a city young or old? There is not much left of the remote past. There is still some baroque here and there, notably in the white exuberance of the Theatiner Church. Then there is the more graceful rococo of the Cuvilliés Theater, an eighteenth-century jewel in white, red, and gold—the pride of the city. The citizens dismantled it, hid it, and reinstalled it in a different place after the war, as its former site had been bombed out. Statues of mad kings, patrons of the arts, stand on squares bearing their name. The Residenz is full of curious things to see, and the Deutsches Museum meticulously displays its seemingly endless treasures to all viewers.

I set out in the icy wind along the Ludwigstrasse, past the balcony from which Hitler used to harangue his Brown Shirts, architecturally a copy of the Loggia dei Lanzi in Florence. It was Sunday. Pedestrians were rare. Mothers bundled up in fur coats waited for the green light to signal *Gehen* (go) before they crossed the street with their baby carriages. I got as far as the Arch of Triumph and then continued into the Schwabing district. What has remained of that famous center of culture and life, rebuilt anew on the ruins? Where are the Rilkes and Georges, Wedekind, the Manns, Ibsen, Däubler, Kurt Eisner, Gundolf, and all the others? Where are *Simplicissimus*, the journalists, caricaturists, political leaders, philosophers, the painters and their models—that whole world which scandalized the Philistines and shocked the bourgeoisie? Nameless streets. . . . Yet examples of the old ornaments that have survived the

16

air raids—volutes, flower decorations, friezes, gro-
tesques, corbels, balconies, cornices—still represent
the richest museum of a style that originated here and
then spread in every direction, even to Italy, in de-
cidedly more provincial forms. This manner, mingled
with a hundred other heterogeneous elements, is
perhaps far from dead. It has become more abstract,
with flowery and stylized aestheticism, with a sche-
matic and ornamental lessening of all the intertwining
curves that abound in Wagner and Rilke and
D'Annunzio—yes, and even in Kandinsky and
Picasso.

The great parks shuddered with the cold now that
the beer festivals were over. Watching over them was
that maternal giant Bavaria, bloated with countless
beers of time out of mind, fat, smug, bulging, affably
pachydermous. Everything was in order, everything
moved along at a leisurely pace—but without the
blatant wealth of other parts of Germany. This is
obviously still a predominantly peasant region based
on traditional economy, with no big industry. But
everywhere there were wide empty spaces, places
cleared of rubble, replaced by new structures in
metal and glass, shops and bookstores with books
from all countries, bright spots meant to be temporary
but fated to last a long time. The largest square in the

center of the city, packed with rows of closely parked cars, was but the greatest of these empty spaces left by the war. The interior of the Cathedral has also been rebuilt on the ruins, with the cold and pedantic techniques of modern museums. Visitors to the Cathedral follow a set route, indicated by signs, arrows, and notices in three languages: "This is a house of worship, not a thoroughfare." Cardinal Faulhaber's tomb lies in the crypt. Opposite the Cathedral is the Central Police Station, a tall and lovely green building sharply outlined against the sky.

So, as I strolled about the city, the hours went by. It was too late to have lunch in a restaurant. To get a bite to eat and then prepare for the lecture I was to give early that evening, I walked back to the Hotel Vierjahreszeiten. In the gray of a northern afternoon the cold light penetrated the dining room of the deserted hotel. I was the only one served. It was one of those days on which one feels like talking to the waiter. Then I discovered that this particular waiter, a short, dark, young man with black eyes and a serious face, flawlessly attired in tails, was an Italian. A friendly soul, he told me all about himself as he served me with the utmost adroitness and deference. He came from Turin, was an orphan, and had gone to school in Cuneo. He had studied agronomy but had been unable to finish the course for lack of money. So far he had had twenty-six occupations. As a waiter, he was obviously first-rate. He had worked in the finest hotels of Europe and now he was here at the Vierjahreszeiten, which has the reputation of being the best hotel in Germany. For six months now he had been studying music, taking lessons from a German music teacher with what he managed to save from his earnings. He wrote songs, both words and melodies—and the German music teacher helped him to transcribe the music. He said he would like to go to the Conservatory because he realized he needed a more basic training. But to do that he would have had to leave his job. "I've worked at all kinds of trades," he told me, "but I've come to realize that for man there is only art. Only art is the real thing. All the others are make-believe. In all of them we have to put on uniforms. I'd like to write too, but writing is too hard. You have to study a lot before you write." He could write novels about all the things he had seen in the big cities, in the night spots of London, for instance: espionage, dope, strikes, love affairs. But he lacked training and technique. Music, on the other hand, was more natural, although it too required lots of work. He had already composed twenty songs, and maybe a music publisher would bring them out. The

19

following night three of his latest songs would be sung at a night club, the Tabu, where new work was often presented. Modestly, yet with deep seriousness, he confessed his ambitions to me. How intent he was on making a career for himself—working on his own, mustering all his energies. I promised him that if I had time I would go and listen to his songs.

I remained alone in the gray silence of late afternoon. No one was with me; even the waiters had disappeared. I thought of the fate of the little people. . . . What should I talk about to the select audience that would listen to me in the white-and-gold rococo theater? I talked about the little people, about our common destiny, about each one of the elements in the infinite dust of men who face life and become free; I talked about the friendship of ordinary human beings who are neither German nor Italian, who are never strangers. I read the story of a child who in a single moment learned both self-expression and freedom—in some trifling yet memorable childish incident; and the story of a young peasant in one of those obscure countries where

> *ignote persone*
> *t'apron fraterni le porte, le tetre*
> *case, l'antica comune miseria.*

unknown persons,
like brothers, open doors for you, open
the gloomy houses, the ancient common
wretchedness.

I told about one of the many unknown men who for
the first time entered upon life and consciousness
through the great drama of a collective movement,
who found in it for the first time both their voices and
their freedom; about a peasant killed for that reason
at dawn of a morning in May, in the midst of the
landlord's grain. And he lay there

con le sue calze bianche sotto il sole

(*Son come pietre dure le parole*
che fan compatto il mondo, l'esistenza
reale, e verde la speranza . . .)

e la sua Madre nera nella stanza.

with his boots white beneath the sun

(They are like hard rocks—the words
that bring the world together, make
existence real and hope ever green . . .)

and his dark Mother in the room.

After my lecture the evening ended with a dinner given me by my German friends, who received me with genuine warmth. They took me to a famous artists' restaurant, where we ate roebuck and huge *Salzburger Nockerln*. Here, within the old wood-paneled walls, were the city's intellectuals: large sturdy faces, heads like Dürer's prophets that seemed crammed with ideas. The restaurant was full, eyes sparkled, people talked, a steady hum—gay and childlike—filled the air. Munich was eight hundred years old. We at our table, with our faces, may have seemed a hundred times younger.

A great city is made up of many superimposed layers. If you dig beneath the surface, it appears different; and every definition seems to elude one endlessly. Where shall we stop, in this flight of time? Which counts more, the surface or the dark layers beneath? History or the fate of individuals? Personalities or the nameless mass? I had met the personalities; I knew them. But what about the ordinary people—what about their lives?

The next day I scanned the faces of the pedestrians as they passed me on the streets hastening through the cold. They were middle-class and peasant

faces of a calm and sleepy region; faces without
violent expressions, without passionate gleams in
their eyes; reserved, heavy-set faces with regular
features. But around five in the afternoon I came out
of the Alte Pinakothek after having spent several
hours in that museum. Bone-weary and hungry, I
entered a restaurant near the Cathedral noted for its
wide variety of sausages and *Würstel*. Then, all of a
sudden, I found these faces different—as if liberated.
Seated at rustic-style tables on chairs with high
wooden backs, middle-aged women were eating sausages and drinking beer. They were completely absorbed in these pleasures of the mouth and stomach,
without any feeling of self-restraint. They were not
eating: they devoured, ingested, consumed, swal-
lowed, chewed, ground, and breathed, like tremendous silkworms completely enclosed in pure voracity.
Their flabby pink flesh was tinged with all the nu-
ances of red and purple; their noses shone; their eyes
shone; their blond curls peeked out beneath their
hats; their cheeks sagged asymmetrically; their
bloated bodies seemed determined to spread beyond
their clothes; their flaccid hands, covered with rings,
seized the heaped-up treasures of food like possessive
claws. Meanwhile they talked, without pausing between one mouthful and another. They laughed

freely and gaily. They were enjoying themselves thoroughly. By their side sat fat dogs wearing coats hooked at the neck. Opposite them, their daughters and their fiancés—slender, blond, and quite handsome—gazed tenderly at each other; but they too, like their mothers, were already devouring and consuming the food. Yet all of them, despite this gay animal-like freedom, still had something lackluster and frightened about them, as if anything not on the dinner plate were incomprehensible and terrifying.

I had seen those faces a short while before. They are the faces in the superb pictures by the earliest German painters, the lesser names as well as the great ones—from Stephan Lochner to von Kulmbach, to the Master of the "Pollinger Tablets," to Martin Schongauer, Hans Baldung, and even Altdorfer, Cranach the Elder, Dürer, and Grünewald. All those magnificent paintings—each in its own way—are extraordinarily realistic. The first image of man they gave to their people was a realistic one, strongly expressive of their feelings, and altogether lacking in what is called "ideal beauty." Perhaps, I thought, as I watched my insatiable female neighbors, these people even today feel so free from any restraints that they are not afraid of ugliness, fatness, deformity, and old age. Perhaps they allow their bodies to be dispropor-

tionate and distorted, without feeling any shame or
fear or complexes about it, because from the outset
their painters never created for them a criterion of
beauty, some standard form which could become a
model and a common tie, even to those not aware of
it. Raphael's "Madonna" hanging in a cheap reprint
above the bed of an Italian peasant woman instills in
her a measure of beauty without her realizing it. The
great German painters have given no other model to
conform to except naked reality or the distortion that
comes from violent emotion. Hence Germany's ancient anarchic freedom has remained without the
usual restraints of form. Expressionism, from its
origins, was inner protest and violence on the part of
the individual. These gluttonous women, revealing
their passion for food, certainly felt peace and harmony. They felt absolved, without guilt, and, perhaps,
very beautiful.

(I I I)

I LEFT these final images of the day in the glaring street lights at dusk before the Cathedral. Evening was drawing on. The ladies at the tables, corpulent afternoon apparitions, were but the middle-class vanguard of a hidden nighttime army.

I set out, as I had promised, for the Tabu in Schwabing, where I expected to hear the songs of the waiter-musician. There I found friends and acquaintances with whom I had made an appointment, and a group of Italian students—young men and women—who were studying in the various schools of the University of Munich. Among them I met one young man, short, shy, reserved, to whom I immediately took a liking when I noticed with what keen insight he observed persons and things. He revealed a warm and lively interest in everything around him. A Venetian, born of a poor family, he was a nephew of a saintly Pope. He proved to be an invaluable companion and interpreter for me, for he had the ability to make immediate contact with other human beings.

The Tabu was a night club with artistic pretensions. A sign outside read that on Mondays it presented "the theater of those unknown." At a given hour after the dancing, the performers would appear before the audience, who were seated at tables. These beginners would sing their own songs or perform their numbers accompanied on the piano or by a noisy little orchestra. When we arrived, the participants were waiting in a little side room. There we found our waiter-musician in evening dress and brought him back to our table. His eyes shone with suppressed excitement. He urged us to pay attention only to the melody when he sang. He would sing as well as he could, but he wasn't a singer; he had never studied singing. He had a long wait before the tryouts began, and to overcome his restlessness, he danced with a plump German girl whose rosy cheeks contrasted with his pale face—only his ears, red from tension, showed any color. Finally the dancing ended. In the middle of the hall, the master of ceremonies made a very long speech that was half serious and half funny. Between jokes and clowning he explained the cultural importance of the Tabu's presentation of youthful talent in Munich, cradle of the arts. After he finished his speech, the artists took over. But the dancing resumed between each appearance of a performer. Our young man from Turin was first. He sang two Italian songs and one German number. He sang with all his heart, with passion, seriousness, and will power, with the deep-rooted sincerity of someone who had faith in work and, at bottom, in the value of man. He was stirred by his own singing; his dark eyes moistened despite his efforts to remain impassive. How deeply he believed in his lonely undertaking! In his songs there was a little of all these emotions, and some things of the imagination as well. There was also his feeling for art, for love, and for Italy. Here, we felt, was a human life expressing itself as well as it could. The least we could do was applaud. And since the performers' abilities were to be judged according to the votes of the audience, we voted for him by writing his name on little slips of paper that had been handed to us. After him came other singers, instrumentalists, monologuists, imitators—a bedlam of emaciated-looking, hoarse-voiced, squealing, thumping novices.

We did not wait for the end, not even for the result of the balloting. It was late, and I wanted to spend the rest of the evening in one of the famous *Bierstuben* of popular tradition, places famed in all conventional stories and reminiscences for their endless collective drinking bouts in which thousands of beer drinkers were said to indulge in loud, unconfined, raucous, powerful, yet orderly gaiety. What I found there was altogether different—a completely different and almost incredible world of rejection and desperate alienation.

At midnight we entered the Hofbräuhaus, biggest of Munich's great beer halls. This was where the first Brown Shirts sat at tables in the 1920's listening to the fanatical speeches of the young Hitler. The huge rooms, formerly stalls, intersected one another like the passageways of an abandoned hospital or poorhouse. The place was virtually deserted. Just then, I was told, the people were economizing because of the Christmas season. The beer hall was about to close for the night. A few late customers lingered: workingmen, clerks, poor people, women overdressed or with too little on, their faces florid from too much beer or wan and scrawny with weariness. Waitresses and barmaids, wearing soiled aprons like attendants at a Turkish bath, passed by with mops and pails of dirty water, clearing away the mountains of mugs bearing the blue letters HB. In the corners, on the beer-stained floor, they changed their stockings.

A group of last-ditch drinkers grumbled among themselves about the level of the beer in the glasses. "It's all foam," they asserted.

An official dressed in military uniform, replete with stripes and ribbons and metal buttons, quickly came over. I could see beneath the visor of his cap that he had the features of a hard-faced bureaucrat. "The beer is at the proper level," he said, thus laying down the law. "I wear a uniform and I'm from the Liquor Board. So I know what I'm talking about. There's nothing more to be said. Quiet now!"

The drunkards were silent.

In a corner at one of the long tables, there was a woman by herself, sitting on a bench against the wall. She was young but her face seemed ageless. It was a broad and coarse face, with grayish complexion, cruel little eyes deeply sunken and squinting beneath heavy eyelids, a flattened nose, protruding cheekbones, a twisted mouth, and widely spaced, misshapen teeth. Her dirty-blond hair came down over her face. She was wrapped in a kind of green soldier's coat, buttoned up to the neck, and wore old down-at-the-heels shoes. She drank her beer with grimaces of disgust. Every one of her gestures was violent and hostile—like some amorphous bundle shaken by movements of inner repulsion. But nestling in her hair, like a flag, was an enormous pink ribbon bow.

I looked at her. Not even a great actress could make herself up to convey such a total picture of degradation. I tried to engage her in conversation. She reacted dully, reluctantly. I invited her to play the "friendship game," which is played as follows: Each player takes one end of a pretzel with his little finger and pulls until the pretzel comes apart. The one left holding the shorter piece pays for the beer. I knew how to lose the game by pulling hard on the pretzel. Before a fresh stein of beer the girl began to talk— or rather grunt. Meanwhile her escort sat down beside her, a puny, weasel-faced postal clerk who interrupted only to hold forth on the value of the mark and the high cost of living in Germany. She came from East Berlin, she told me, was twenty-two, and worked as a cook in another beer hall. Her hours were from five in the morning until one the following morning; her pay, a hundred and twenty marks a month, board, and free beer. She slept at an aunt's house.

She had a four-year-old son, but didn't know where he was and didn't want to see him. The child's father was dead. As she delivered her staccato sentences, her hands gestured with disgust and her face expressed complete revulsion. It was as if her very words, as they emerged from her broken-down mouth, had to traverse an ocean of nausea, weariness, and horror. The next day, she said, was her day off. But she would go to work just the same. She would go to the beer hall because there she could drink as much as she pleased—beer and wine and lemonade. . . .

"Haven't you ever thought about going back to Berlin?"

"*Pfui!* Here a person can drink!"

It was closing time. We walked out into the medieval darkness, past old houses and an ancient windmill. We headed for a prosperous beer cellar in the prosperous heart of the city—the Donisel, or Damsel's. It was jammed when we got there, with an odd assortment of human beings: hard-faced war veterans scarred or crippled in one way or another, with glass eyes or artificial limbs; white-collar workers; students with slashed faces sitting silently and motionlessly for hours with their girl friends in front of beer steins,

holding hands and gazing into space with lost looks
of nebulous romanticism; and solitary figures brood-
ing in somber impenetrable gloom. One flight up, an
inept accordion player was seated at the head of the
stairs. The whining of his instrument was carried over
loudspeakers and resounded everywhere. Standing
stiffly beside him was the Liquor Board inspector, so
fat that he almost blocked our passage. He scanned
us like a top sergeant as we threaded our way around
him. Below, the customers were more diversified,
many of them ordinary workers. Those sitting at
tables drank with their neighbors as if with old
friends, yet usually they were total strangers. Everyone sat down wherever he could when a seat was
vacated. The faces seemed frozen by some unknown
terror. Eyes full of fright or fanatical fever stared
straight ahead and appeared to see nothing but an
inner desert. I asked myself whether this was only
because of too much beer drinking. Or was it, rather,
an intimate horror, a categorical rejection, an anguish
impossible to define?

I sat down at the corner of a table where there
was an empty seat. Near me was a woman who
looked like an older sister of the Berlin girl in the
Hofbräuhaus. The same dull and contemptuous brut-
ishness, the same brusque and distorted movements,

the hair in disarray. . . . Next to me was another woman, a brunette with too much make-up, a member of the same nameless and dismal family. To my left was a small skinny woman with the yellowish complexion of a consumptive, painted eyelids, bloodless lips, and tiny, dark, flashing eyes. Provoked by the men at the table, she retorted that she didn't like the way they made love nowadays. There was too much perversion all around. She was a cook from Ulm. She had come to Munich because it was a holiday and she wanted company. In the beer hall, of course, not in bed. In bed she preferred to sleep alone.

"Men don't want to be disturbed, you know. They want to be left alone."

"You'd better leave *us* alone," an old man sitting opposite her replied with a laugh. He had a serious face and, with his eyeglasses, looked a little like a professor. But he was a retired worker living on a pension. Amiably he explained that he liked to spend his evenings here. At home he had no one.

So the talk turned to loneliness, and then work; everyone spoke his piece. I turned to a young fellow who was sitting silently next to the cook. He had a small stunted body with a tiny pointed head. One of his hands was wrapped in dirty bandages. When I asked him what his trade was, he looked at me with terrified eyes and broke his silence with only a laconic "My trade? Beer—and women."

At a nearby table three women were in the midst of animated conversation. Two of them were plump and middle-aged, with curly blond hair beneath their oddly tilted hats. Their faces were shiny, their fingers covered with rings, and necklaces hung around their necks. They resembled battered old hulks of boats that had been repatched and repainted and now were resting, for a short time, in the snug refuge of the harbor. The third woman, whom I could see only from the back, wore slacks and a long jacket made of some coarse and heavy material. Her dirty-blond hair was cut very short and she gestured like a man. But when I sat down at their table I saw that her face was already old. Yet it bore traces of a former beauty. Her fingers were slender and elegant-looking, and she had a certain rather striking grace, even in the harshness of her phrases and gestures. At first she eyed me coldly and almost hostilely. She complained that they had refused to serve her any more drinks. I intervened on her behalf and ordered another beer for her. Then she began to talk—disjointedly, incoherently, as if revolving in an irregular orbit around some obscure center in which, judging from her words and glances, there resided extreme violence and despair. She expressed herself in cultured language, in pungent, expressive sentences. One felt there was something in her trying to emerge —a sorrow, a hate, a contempt, a wound. She fished in her handbag and took out a small document that had been given to her by one of the tourist agencies: it praised her ability as a guide to one of the castles in the Bavarian mountains. Now it was wintertime; the castle was closed. Her job lasted for six months.

"And the other six months?" I asked.

She looked at me with all the disgust a human being could have for life. "The other six months? Beer."

Little by little her story unfolded. It came out in bits and pieces, frequently interrupted and then resumed, and always orbiting around that empty and agonizing center which held her there on that bench, at that hour of the night. An actress in her younger days, she had played in Max Reinhardt's theater and had known Brecht. Then time passed; misfortunes came. Suddenly she whispered to me: "Everything that's German is nothing but hatred," and stared at her beer glass. "Don't believe what you see," she continued. "They all have smiles on their faces, but it's nothing but hate. They're all getting rich and look human, but they're the same as they were before.

My brothers were Nazis, terrible Nazis; they're Nazis today. My father, even my father (he was born in Russia, my mother came from the Rhineland) was a Nazi. On that horrible night when they wrecked the homes of the Jews, he went out to smash the windows in Clara Zetkin's house. My husband was a Jew; we had a little girl. One night the Nazis came to our house. They grabbed my husband and beat me up. They took him away. They laughed and said to me: 'We'll bring him back to you in ten minutes.' Later, because of the war and because I was poor, I had to leave my little girl with my brother. My daughter doesn't know that her father was Jewish. If I told her, my brother would throw her out of the house."

The beer glasses were empty; the world was empty. It was three a.m., and the beer hall was closing for two hours. The customers cleared out. All the acquaintances who had come with me had remained at another table while I was talking to the woman. Sitting in a glass-partitioned booth, they were busy tasting various kinds of sausages. Now they left me and returned home. The only one who stayed was the Venetian student. We stopped beneath the portico of the Donisel, not sure where we would go next. The motley crew of drinkers had left the beer hall. The hunchback accordion player, his face thin and jaundiced, was the last to leave. He told us about another beer hall, which stayed open until five—and then the one we had just left would reopen. "There," he assured us, "you'll feel good. It's not far. There you'll see the last men." We headed toward it in the night.

What drove us, on that last night in Munich, at so late an hour, through streets swept by an icy wind? Perhaps the feeling that there was something else in that nether world I was visiting, something else even more elementary and revealing than the inner loneliness, or the brutalized face of the Berlin cook, or the story of Frida, the woman who couldn't tell her daughter the name and religion of her father, whom the Nazis had murdered.

So I strode along the dark streets with my young Italian friend. And we were disturbed as we thought about the events and the destinies written on the faces that had passed before us; and those terror-stricken eyes, that unconcealed suffering, so openly and genuinely and heartbreakingly laid bare. But Frida had not left us. She had followed and overtaken us. Now she was leading us to the last beer hall, walking arm in arm with us over the deserted sidewalks. "At first I didn't trust you. I didn't like your

38

friends. One of them looked like a Faust on the prowl. And his wife? A mask, a hypocrite. But then I realized that you're not like them."

Now that her initial defenses were down, Frida felt less wary and even friendly toward us. She opened up, confessing her sorrow and crying out her hate—hatred for herself, for her country and the world. This hatred ravaged her yet made her sharp. It possessed some dark clairvoyance that penetrated things and distorted them.

At length we came to the beer hall where, so we had been told, we would find "the last men." At first glance it was a quiet place, without any of the rowdiness or hideous-looking faces bloated from too much beer. The three of us sat down by ourselves at a table. At first I felt that there was really nothing interesting here, that I would have been better off had I gone back to the hotel to sleep instead of staying with this embittered woman who kept on striking the same monotonous note of negation and violence. Frida started talking again, making sarcastic remarks and swearing. "It's three o'clock. This is the hour for beer, the hour of truth. You see those people sitting over there? All of them, on the outside, are fine, respectable people. But look at them! They're nothing but worms—Nazi worms. Where are the men? Are there any? Tell me, are there any men? Men who can fight, who will free you from these worms? Do you know where they are? And what are you doing about it?"

Through the revolving door a well-dressed man entered. He wore an overcoat with a fur collar and had a big cigar in his mouth.

"Look at him: the Power of Money!" Frida labeled him.

The newcomer, with a patronizing gesture, greeted the old cripple sitting there and singing to the accompaniment of his own accordion. He patted the old man on the back and cried: "Hello, Caruso!"

"Did you hear what he said?" Frida asked. "Caruso! That's his language. The language of the Power of Money. Worms!"

At the table next to ours was a massive woman, black-haired, big-busted, with hairy armpits and a hardened, stupid, animal-like face. With her were two elderly men dressed in Bavarian costume, similar to that worn by Italian streetcar conductors, with green leaves sewed on their coat lapels. One of them—I don't know why—attracted my attention. He was pasty-looking, fat, and flabby, with the tired watery eyes of a workingman. His features were vulgar and crude, yet for some obscure reason they aroused my

40

curiosity. The musician approached our table and began singing an old German folksong, *Morgenrot*. ("Dawn, dawn, Your light shines for my too early death. Soon the trumpet will sound And I will have to give up my life.") Frida, resting her arms on our shoulders, sang along with him. Now she was more relaxed in her movements. There was even something affectionate and maternal in them. Others in the place joined in. The melody, barely recognizable and sung out of tune by tired and wheezy voices, reminded me of the Ballad of Mackie Messer and the Soho poor from Brecht's *Threepenny Opera*. I asked the musician to play it.

> *Denn die einen sind im Dunkel*
> *Und die andern sind im Licht*
> *Und man siehe die im Lichte,*
> *Die im Dunkel, sieht man nicht* . . .

For some are in darkness
And others are in light
And you can see those in the light,
But those in the darkness you cannot see . . .

Then, as soon as the musician had begun to play, the man at the next table abruptly got up. He came over to the accordion player with a one-mark coin in his hand. *"I* want to pay," he said in a loud voice. "I want to pay for the song this gentleman requested. That's the right kind of music. I'm paying for it. I'll pay for all the songs this gentleman requests, because the ones he requests are the right ones." Mystified by this action, I told the player to continue and to repeat the refrain.

> *Jenny Towler ward gefunden*
> *Mit 'nem Messer in der Brust . . .*

> Jenny Towler was found
> With a knife in her breast . . .

Then the man got up again, took his stein of beer, and came over to my table. He sat down, put down the stein, and sobbed.

Big tears rolled down his wan cheeks. "I haven't talked to anyone about it yet," he muttered. "I have to talk. I found out today at six o'clock. The police called me and broke the news. My daughter . . . was murdered. She was a whore in Soho. Her pimp stabbed her to death. Nobody knows it yet, only me and my brother who went with me to the police station. I didn't tell them at home. I came here. I couldn't talk.

42

But I saw you looking at me like a man, and I had to
tell you. You looked at me, and asked to have this
music played, the music of the poor people of Soho.
So I had to tell you. She was twenty-one. It's three in
the morning, I couldn't keep quiet any more. And you
looked at me, you asked for the song." The tears fell
silently.

"It's my fault that Erna had her throat slit. I was
too strict with her. Three years ago she was going to
have a baby. I was very strict. Then in her fourth
month she had an abortion. So, after a stay in the
hospital and a bit of trouble with the police, she got a
job as a maid with some English officials in Munich.
Before that she worked in Ingolstadt. Then the English family took her to London. After that she worked
there as a salesgirl. Then when we found out she was
supposed to go to Africa, we understood. My brother
went to London last year to make her come back. But
she didn't come back. Her pimp . . . he cut her
throat. He's a German from Berlin. In Soho."

I murmured vague words of condolence. As if
he had just become aware of a human presence, his
tongue loosened and he began to narrate the story of
his life. He took my hand and made me feel a scar
beneath his thinning hair. "I was in France during
the war. I was in Italy too, in Venice. But I got this

wound at Dunkirk—a fragment of a V-1 that exploded." He took a sip of beer, then pursued his story. He did sign painting and lettering for signs, posters, and handbills. He wasn't a poor man and owned his own business. He was fifty-four years old. At twenty he got married for the first time—to Inge. His son was working in Wolfsburg, at the Volkswagen factory. Then he got a divorce and married Magda. Magda's three children were working in the Nymphenburg porcelain factory. Then he married Resi, who died giving birth to twins. But the woman he loved was Maria, the mother of his murdered daughter, Erna. After the war he met her again, working for the occupation forces and eating potato peels to keep from starving. Then her last daughter was born—she was black. And his beloved Maria went away, and now he was without a woman. During the war he had been a corporal. He was a Catholic—devoted to St. Anselm, St. Conrad, and St. Peter. And Erna was dead.

It was a release, a long retelling volunteered for its own sake, perhaps in order to absolve him of his fate. "I had to tell you my life story. . . . But why? Why France? Why war? Why was I wounded? Why was I so hard on my daughter? Why did my daughter become a whore? Why did she go to Soho? Why was she murdered? Why have I found *ein Mensch*, a man, a human being, who looked at me and made me feel I had to talk to him? This is the man I have to talk to, even though he's not from my country and doesn't know my language. I talk to him and he can't understand me. Why? Whose fault is it? It's God's fault. It's God's fault—because God is Jewish."

It was almost dawn. We could not go on from there. I said good-by to him, expressing the hope that life might give him some reward for his pains. As I left, he ran after me, held me back, then knelt to the ground and kissed my hand.

(I V)

SITTING in a spacious armchair in the lobby of the Vierjahreszeiten, I too felt like one of those big businessmen, protected by layers of fat and indifference, swathed in majestic blue clouds of cigar smoke, who were enthroned there like monarchs and transacted their childish affairs. My last morning in Munich was spent on one of those thrones—with visits, greetings, and conversations that followed one another and overlapped. First a publisher: tall, lean, cultured, impeccably groomed, witty, with only one arm; then journalists, photographers, translators, young intellectuals; and then a famous man of the theater, keenly and authoritatively intelligent, undismayed by old age which caused one of his eyelids

46

to sag and his hands to shake. He was accompanied
by his son, a clever young man, whose face had been
scorched and eaten away by a flame thrower. The
young man was dressed all in black, with black
gloves and high black boots. He looked like an ap-
parition or a ghost—or like a smartly dressed,
lugubrious hunter in the lower world.

While chatting with them I noticed someone cross
the room and come toward me. He was middle-aged,
untidily dressed, tremendous in stature, robust and
broad-shouldered, but slightly bent and somehow con-
tracted and diminished, even with his athletic build.
He had a big head of white hair that fell in smooth
forelocks over his forehead, heightening by contrast
the faded tan of his complexion. Where had I seen
that face? That flattened nose, that small slit of a
mouth, and—set surprisingly in the broad expanse of
his features—those dark and piercing eyes? And that
expression of melancholy irony and wit? Only when
he came closer to my armchair and greeted me by
name did I recognize him. His gestures and tone of
voice suddenly brought him back to me—as if borne
by a gust of wind out of the dense fog of memory. It
was Rainer P., a sculptor I hadn't seen in perhaps
thirty years, not since the prehistoric days of Paris
between the two world wars. He was one of those who

had poured out of all parts of Europe onto the old pavements of the Left Bank, like a wandering band of gypsies, intent on discovering the future in art forms that merged and clashed. I used to see P. at the Montparnasse cafés with Zadkine, Kokoschka, and Soutine; with Russian, Polish, Jewish, and Negro artists; with the surrealists; with all sorts of artists and human beings in that heterogeneous, tormented, effervescent world. The two men with whom he was most friendly were Arp and Brancusi. He felt driven by a passion for political freedom and pure expression. These were his two motives for leaving his native Germany well before Hitler came to power. Despite appearances, Germany, to him, already exuded the stench of death. He could not stand its spirit, its way of life, its false democracy, its traditions, or any of its fundamental traits. He set his hopes of revolution on his statues, which were abstracts in polished stone.

At that time I had been on intimate terms with him. But it was now so long ago—impossible to attempt to recapture it. Our past is made up of a thousand lives, each complete and self-contained in its own world: lives lived and then abandoned, so that one can go on living. An old man with the robustness of an oak once talked to me about this.

Describing the architects and great men of his youth in the tone of one who has remained alone on the mountaintop, Frank Lloyd Wright said to me: "I have seen them come from afar; *a handshake, and they went away*." Apart from his specific genius and advanced age, which lent nobility to his words, this sense of detachment from the past is common to all who have lived a long time; especially those who have lived in various ways and places in a time, like our own, of profound changes. When one of the figures of our past returns, we get a feeling—a thoroughly unjustified feeling, be it said—that time has been violated, as if the returning figure bound us to what was no longer within us, to a nonexistent image of ourselves. So, with an involuntary trace of this resentment along with some of the warmth I had once felt for him, I looked at Rainer.

He had not changed in looks, except that his hair had grown white and there was a bitterer, more sardonic twist to his mouth. His eyes still had the same light I had known—sarcastic and at the same time guileless. After his first fragmentary accounts, full of gaps and hesitations, I realized that he had clung to the ideals of his younger days. He had carried them with him through all the revolutions, rebellions, resistances, jails, exiles, and concentration camps in every country in Europe until finally, after World War II, he had come back to Germany—I wasn't quite sure how. He had returned to the Germany in which he had been born and which, from his earliest youth, he had spurned and rejected. How many times had I heard him, sitting before a *café-crème,* declare that he would never again set foot in his country until after a complete revolution there—a revolution that would turn it inside out like a glove and put on top those who had been at the bottom, and even change its name! Then, with the passage of time, the revolutions in reverse, and the fraying of certainties, he had come back to his place of origin—to Germany. He remained in his native land and was fond of it in spite of himself—as in a homeland he was duty-bound to love, or a prison to which he had grown accustomed. But for having had so much courage—how much discouragement, and how much pain! He had been forced to give up sculpture. To earn a livelihood he had become a designer of modern interiors. But did he really still believe in the ideas and hopes he had so jealously preserved? Perhaps all he believed in now was an abstract and noble-minded loyalty.

He introduced his wife to me. Minna, Rumanian-born, was no longer young but still lovely-looking, blond, slender, silent, reserved, shut up in her thoughts. They had come from Switzerland, had spent a few days here in Munich, and were leaving shortly for Düsseldorf, where they lived. As I had to go the same way for part of my trip, they invited me to ride in their car instead of going by train. Meanwhile the Venetian student had joined us. He had not slept. After taking me back to my hotel at four in the morning, he had returned to the beer hall to be with the father of the girl murdered in Soho. He had spent the rest of the night with the bereaved parent—with his empty grief, his guilty God, and his racist metaphysic of loneliness. Then the two of them had returned to the Donisel as soon as it reopened and had drunk more beer until it was broad daylight. Finally the young Italian had taken the man home to a distant suburb, whence he had hastened back in order to see me off. He agreed readily to go with us for a part of the journey. So, after my last good-bys to my Munich acquaintances, the four of us got into the car.

Good-by Munich, Bavaria, beer halls, rococo, *Baumkuchen,* kings, peasants, mountains, Schwabing, Wagnerism, and *Sezession!* Shortly after noon we set out toward the beautiful Germany of the black forests and ancient cities, for the rich Germany of industry and labor. As we rode toward the Munich suburbs, our Volkswagen, its engine buzzing and humming, seemed like some primal insect identical with thousands of others swarming around us. Traffic was so well regulated and violating the rules of the road so unthinkable that, of course, accidents were numerous. We witnessed one as we left the city. It occurred so slowly and absurdly that it had a dream-like quality. A truck made a turn at a very slow speed, crossing the tracks in the middle of the road. A streetcar approached and slowed down until it almost came to a stop. A passenger car moved at a very moderate speed in the opposite direction. We saw the three vehicles approach one another. I don't know which of the three was at fault; all of them could easily have stopped. Instead, all three kept going until there was the inevitable crash. Each of them was stubbornly confident that the law was on its side, a confidence deeper than their imagination.

The weather was calm and gray. Now we were in the country, passing neat-looking villages, modest low-cost homes, and small factories. We were heading for the *Autobahn* to Stuttgart, with a detour at Dachau. I asked for this when I saw that name on one of the road signs. After a moment's hesitation Rainer generously consented. We stopped at a drab-looking village with tall dark houses and inquired about the road to the former concentration camp. They told us about a nearby camp. But that *Lager* was not Dachau; it was a new refugee camp. Speaking with the controlled enthusiasm of someone trying to convince himself, Rainer told me how the German Government was providing for these immigrants, how there was work for everybody, with steady jobs and good pay. In a few years Germany had developed its industries tremendously and had rebuilt its cities. Now there was no poverty there. Driving along tree-lined streets, we came at last to a bleak bare plain. As if the weather itself sought to re-create an image that history had made, all of a sudden the gray sky turned black. An icy wind began to blow and a raging snowstorm was upon us. We were in the middle of a kind of drained, treeless marshland, swept by shrieking winds. Slowly we kept close to a wall that seemed to go on forever. Through openings in the wall we caught sight of barracks. It was Dachau.

We continued to hug the wall until we came to the entrance of a little garden, with patches of grass and saplings that swayed in the wind. Here we got out. The snow penetrated our clothes, entered our eyes, and almost prevented us from seeing. This place was like a public park, like the flower beds around a rural railroad station or those in a cemetery. A stone tablet commemorated the millions who died there, beneath this grass still green. Along the paths were signs that read: "Here pitchforks were used." "Here they killed with revolvers." "This ditch was used to drain off the blood." We entered a barracks quarter on which was written: "Showers," climbing what had been the last stairs in the life of so many human beings. These were the gas chambers. Bare concrete, with death vents in the ceiling. Off to one side were the ovens: two brick ovens that seemed unusually modest and primitive for the work they did. Opposite them, in another lesser barracks, was the first and oldest of the crematoria, which for a long time had been sufficient. It looked like a bakery oven. How small and simple were the instruments of the artisans of death! The drainage ditches for blood were like those dug by a farmer with his hoe to irrigate his fields. These tiny plots of grass, so trim and neat, these gravel paths, were still, one felt, a site of human sacrifice—one very near to us yet terribly archaic. Rainer murmured to me: "My wife, Minna, never came here. Her mother, her father, her whole family, were wiped out here." Dry-eyed, she looked mutely at these well-kept lawns.

54

Beyond a green gate commenced the expanse of the field barracks. A soldier stood motionless on guard amid the whirling snow. For Minna's sake I did not want to prolong our visit. So we went back again along the interminable wall. At an opening leading to some streets within the cluster of barracks buildings there was a sign: *Gute Küche* (Good Cooking). I saw a woman, her head wrapped in a shawl, hurry across the snow carrying a pail and a bundle of fagots. Here and there yellowish lights came on in the miniature barracks windows. The camp was completely inhabited. I did not want to stop, yet something drew me toward that somber place. Leaving my friends in the car with an "Oh, I'll just stay a few minutes!" I started out with the Venetian student. We walked among the huts where those about to die had lived. A little girl came out of a door. I asked her if we could go in. After knocking, I went in and found myself in a tiny room separated from the rest of the barracks by a wooden partition. In the rear, beneath the window where snow was piling up, was a cot covered with tattered bedclothes. On the cot two skeletons were seated: two men with huge, cavernous, colorless eyes, wracked with fever and gaunt with anguish, their skin wrinkled and flabby and pale yellow, their hands on their knees, wearing ill-fitting

55

trousers and frayed sweaters over their hollow chests. They sat there staring motionlessly.

Was this sight something real—or a product of my imagination, a dream? There was also a woman in the room. Gray, ageless, she was bending over a wooden cradle set on the floor and wrapping a baby in gray blankets. The infant, four months old, was starved-looking. The room contained a table, a stove, a chair, and a few metal pots. I didn't know how to talk to these people. But the one who looked most haggard and beaten and skeletonlike politely invited me to sit down. Then he talked.

They were refugees, "expellees"; their name was Sperling. The entire Dachau camp was filled with refugees. The woman was his wife. They came from eastern Silesia. The other man, his brother-in-law, didn't live here; he was in another camp, not far from Munich. Today he was visiting them. He had a job. "But I can't work. I'm sick. I should go to a sanatorium, but I can't afford it. They won't listen to me; they don't believe I'm sick. Here anyone who is weak is guilty. They give us relief: a hundred and twenty marks per person per month. Not everyone in the *Lager* here is poor. There are poor and rich. Some carry on businesses; some have a TV set and a car. We're waiting for a house. They promised us one.

We're waiting. But you have to have two thousand marks to get one. I can't work, I haven't got the money, I'll never have it. I weigh eighty pounds. Look at me. Touch me." He rose. He was a lanky man. When he turned up a trouser leg all I could see was the outline of his knee bones between the femur and the tibia. There was no flesh beneath the creased skin. I realized, by contrast, what a monstrous giant of flesh and blood and vital energy I was. My shoulders touched the two walls of the little room; I spanned it and filled it completely, like an unlawful presence from another world.

"In Silesia I was a house painter. We were seven brothers. I was the youngest. My father said I was lazy and sent me off to war. The Russians made me a prisoner. Now I've been here for eleven years. The prisoners who were here before were not worse off than us." His dull voice broke; he began to sob. Yet today was a big day for him, because today he had won five hundred marks in the football pool. That was why his brother-in-law had come to see him. (Now I took a good look at the brother-in-law: the same haunted look, the inhuman gray of the *Lager*. But he was not just a bony skeleton and when he talked his voice had a livelier and more vigorous sound.) What should he do with the five hundred marks? The family was discussing it. It wasn't enough money to pay for the house, or for the sanatorium either. Should he use it to buy medicines? Or coal for the stove instead? Or for food? Or some other necessities? This unexpected stroke of luck did not bring joy to their hearts. In their world there was no hope. "What should we do? Go back *there?* Maybe. At least there, so they say, there aren't the big differences there are here, even here in the camp. They don't have either rich or poor. But how can I go back? I don't even know if my home town still exists."

I left the barracks. The snowstorm had died down. Other black ghosts flitted among the huts and over the frozen mud. So the world of concentration camps was still present, and not only in the memory and conscience? Rainer and Minna had patiently waited for us in the Volkswagen, its windows coated with ice. We dropped the student off at a nearby village station, where he could take a train to Munich. (Later he wrote me that he had gone back to Dachau and that the family we had seen was an exceptional case, perhaps due to alcoholism or t.b. Yet that had been a true image. Not for nothing was it the only one we saw.)

Now we drove westward along the superb *Autobahn*, past tranquil villages and peaceful forests, in a

gentle and rolling landscape. A pale sun began to
sink over the horizon in a patch of blue sky among
the clouds. The highway was covered with a thin
layer of ice, causing cars to skid. Finally the sky
darkened and filled with cold stars as we entered the
sixteenth-century streets of the city of Augsburg.

(V)

A S W E entered Augsburg that evening, the dark and deserted streets revealed a charm and ancient harmony that had been either preserved or rediscovered. We felt a sense of permanent order and unity as though one mind alone had presided over the shaping of the entire city and its life. Leaving the car in the ice-covered courtyard of a modest hotel, we went down the main street past the Fugger Houses, now closed because of the late hour but lit up by Christmas trees and stars. The oldest houses were themselves like trees, sharply outlined triangular fir trees; they were colored, decorated, and festooned, and grew gradually narrower as one mounted from floor to floor. Huddled together as in a forest, they soared upward toward the wintry sky. Near them was the stately building of the Rathaus, a product of the Fuggers' genius and one of the most remarkable monuments of Renaissance architecture.

Every window, every column, every architrave of the Rathaus has the most proper and almost academic classical proportions, yet they all convey a vertical effect. Everything presses upward in a way that transforms this architecture and marks it with very strong traces of Gothic, thus giving it a strange flavor, a color that is modern and even contemporary. So too, elsewhere, these traces modify the baroque of the other Fugger houses and of the churches and palaces, fusing to perfection diverse periods and cultures. The great two-headed eagle perches, as if in its nest on some rocky crag, on the rear façade of the Rathaus, towering over the Christmas trees between the stalls of the market place and the old shops of the artisans.

But at this hour, in this bitter cold, in this atmosphere of small-town peace and quiet, the only place to which we could turn for warmth and shelter was one of the beer halls. We tried several; they were quiet and half deserted. In one of them, Rainer, after ordering a round of beer, told us shyly, almost reluctantly, something of his life. He talked about the

Spanish War, in which he had fought with the International Brigades against Moors, Italians, and Germans; of the final exodus from Spain, the crossing of the border at Port Bou, and of the Spanish poet Gustavo Machado, who had left his homeland behind, only to die; of the French concentration camps, forerunners of the others still to come; of Le Vernet, where Corsican corporals had revealed the full fury of their sadism and where he had found again an old surrealist friend, Max Ernst; and of his flight after the fall of France. These were stories of the end of Europe, by one of the millions of eyewitnesses and participants. Then, I can't recall why, he turned to the partisan war in the Balkans, in Yugoslavia and Greece. He told of other jails, sufferings, struggles, and servitudes. Then victory . . . and with victory doubts about what the truth really was. "I've always hewed to the line," said Rainer, as if talking to himself. But little by little hardships increased and wore down one's resistance. All of a sudden things became real, and different from what one had imagined they would be. There were the annoyances of bureaucratic machines, of a political policy that had gained the day; and there was the need to live after so much constant fighting.

He had found Minna in one of the *Lager*, right

after liberation. She was then a mere girl, a living skeleton; she had survived. Minna listened and half-smiled but said nothing. Were there still somewhere simple, happy young girls, dreaming of white dresses and orange blossoms, and of the sounds of an organ in church?

So we went on discussing and exchanging ideas. Then we lapsed into silence as we got ready to leave the last beer hall. All at once someone rushed over to our table. He was a very short man with a round head and dressed in worker's clothes; and he spoke quickly, volubly, almost frantically. Greeting us with sweeping gestures and a flood of words, as if we were old friends, he said that the next day was his birthday. (Probably, I thought, that was the way he usually got treated to a glass of beer.) With his beer glass before him, his garrulousness brooked no interruption. We couldn't even open our mouths. His talk was like a rampaging river, rushing on with disconnected and scatterbrained words of utter stupidity and exhibitionism. He was fifty-three, a railroad worker; his job was testing the brakes on the trains (he went "Bang! Bang!" with an imaginary hammer). He was a devout Catholic with five daughters and one son. It had taken him an hour and a half to make the latter. An inner voice told him that if he had gone about it more quickly the baby would have been born a girl. But by choosing the right time, and by showing patience, it had turned out to be a boy. Germany was doing all right—there was peace and there was Adenauer. "I carried Adenauer's bag when he went through here. We're lucky there's Adenauer and Eisenhower too. I carried Eisenhower's bag too. Adenauer and Eisenhower, yessir!"

His speech raced on as he repeated the rhymed names. When he heard that I was Italian, he shouted: *"Bella Italia!* Mussolini! I went to Italy, on a pilgrimage to Rome, to see Mussolini. Adenauer, Eisenhower, and Mussolini!" My curiosity aroused by this dubious pilgrimage and by the wanderings of his confused mind, I asked him how Mussolini had been dressed. "All in white, and on his head he had a big white miter."

"But then the person you saw wasn't Mussolini. Maybe you mean the Pope?"

"Yes, the Pope! Mussolini! Adenauer! Eisenhower!" As we were going out, he gave each of us a flawless military salute and loudly clicked his heels together. So we left him to his comic devices.

Meanwhile one of Rainer's cousins had joined us and invited us to spend the rest of the evening at his house. He was a little man who, despite his age, had

preserved the youthful and almost too perfect hand-
someness of some Germans. Pale and light-
complexioned, he had glistening hair, a pointed chin,
and a bitter mouth. He was an intellectual. Minna
assured me he was cultured and refined, endowed
with unusual artistic talents, which he had deliberately renounced after a brilliant start. I read in his
keen sad eyes the story of a tragedy that was not his
alone. It was like Rainer's and that of so many others,
the tragedy of a whole generation that had endured
too much, experienced too many humiliations and
lost hopes, known violence and their fathers' betrayal.
Hence their refusal to live, out of loyalty to something
they felt could no longer be true. In this man's case
the melancholy withdrawal into self had not resulted
in bitterness, but rather in a resigned human gentle-
ness, in friendly courtesy, in amiability, in an interest
in culture so desperate there was something dismal
about it. To get to his house we left the center of
town and drove through the new sections, impersonal
and ugly, where modern buildings were under construction. The hours went by as we drank beer and ate
black bread with cheese, discussing the lost problems
of the old Central European intelligentsia and their
present-day brood: Beckett, Ionesco, so many others.
. . . And, of course, we talked about Picasso.

"Picasso is like Bach. He has the same, exactly the same, counterpoint," Rainer's cousin said to me. He repeated this again as we were about to go. I didn't agree with him, but it was too late to recommence a fruitless discussion. Yet he insisted on proving his point to me. He had an amazingly rich record collection of Bach's cello suites—No. 1, in G major, and No. 2, in D minor, played magnificently by Pablo Casals. It was a unique opportunity to hear these rare recordings. They are among the most perfect things in the world. So we turned back from the door, took off our overcoats, and listened to that sublime music. At three in the morning the playing was over. Our host went out to open the outside gate and escorted us to the ice-covered car. In the howling wind, beneath the austere wintry sky, he was still shouting to me as the engine started up: "Counterpoint! Watch for the counterpoint. And remember: Bach's counterpoint is exactly the same as Picasso's."

In the cold sun of a winter's morning, thinly veiled by a light blue haze, we drove back to the old streets of Augsburg city, so different by daylight. The subtle hues of the façades and roofs gave a physical sense of the stratification of emotions that had not been pro-

66

foundly altered by time. They offered evidence of loving care and attention to little things, a brightening of the modest instruments of the spirit. Green vegetables, turnips, red apples, and potatoes filled the market with a riot of color; then there were barrels of sauerkraut, and plucked yellow geese. We entered the Fuggerei, the housing project built by the Fuggers for the workers in the 1500's with a concept of social relations that was already modern and bourgeois. It is a kind of preview or anticipation of the latest and most advanced stage of neocapitalism. We see this today in the most highly developed industrial nations, where some of the enlightened industrialists hire the best architects to design living quarters for their workers. But the houses in the Fuggerei are nicer than our best and even more comfortable, despite their old age.

The Fuggerei is an enclosed area with several intersecting inner streets. It has the atmosphere of peace and sanctuary of a large monastery. Entering one of the homes, we were welcomed by an old lady who had been living there for thirty years with her husband, a retired worker. She showed us the well-polished wooden walls, the stove, the neat furniture, and the vases of flowers. Rent is a mere token payment. The Fugger management, after four hundred years, still governs the area. Entrance into the community is still a privilege; one must not only show need but give guarantees of good character. There is a long waiting list, and families must wait several years before even hoping to be accepted.

Going along the main street, dominated by the white church of St. Ulrich, we came to the Fountain of Hercules. Then we visited the Fugger Houses, all of them perfectly restored since the war. The courtyards and Renaissance cloisters are inspiring examples of the architecture of the first great bankers, a legacy of humane social relations. I followed some trucks with a golden goose painted on their sides until I reached an old house. There, through a large window, I noticed an enormous dome-shaped apparatus in bright copper. On the front, a sign in Gothic script said that this factory, "The Golden Goose," had been in operation on this same spot since 1300. Tall gaunt women and apprentices bundled in coarse woolens went in and out through tiny doors leading to the courtyard. Both groups, in gestures, coloring, and facial expression, resembled figures of the earliest Middle Ages.

The sun was now high in the sky, and we left for Ulm.

(VI)

RIDING in our Volkswagen through the peaceful winter countryside, past broad meadows and spotless unassuming peasant villages, past plains and valleys, and over hills, we peered at the green and gray horizon flecked here and there with big dark patches of woods. Suddenly we came to a great river. The waters of this river were green, dense, deep; with a force and impact that must, one felt, carry it far along. We were at Ulm. It was the Danube.

It was the first time I had seen that famous river. Its name alone, and that mighty swelling and churning of its waters, had a fascination that held me for a long time on the bridge. At my side Minna watched the ever moving liquid mass and remained silent. I followed her sad eyes: they were of the same green as

69

the river. Without moving they seemed to go with the current toward the little town far to the east which would see the same waters that now passed under our gaze. These thoughts and feelings made me want to throw something in the water that would be borne all the way to the sea. The only thing I could find in my pocket was an empty matchbox. We watched it drop over the railing and fall below, until finally it came lightly to rest on the water, like a microscopic raft, and began its long journey.

Waters move; thoughts, ideas, feelings, move. That which is born in one place turns up elsewhere, whither it is carried by the impetus, or inner destiny, of its movement. Astrologers symbolize the constellation Pisces by means of two fishes facing in opposite directions; and from this opposition they infer the dual and tormented nature, the ambivalences and violent ambitions, of anyone born under this star. So Germany is marked, as if by two immense fishes, by the two largest rivers in Europe, the Rhine and the Danube, flowing in opposite directions, east and west. Can we conceive of an astrology of national characteristics as well as one for individuals? If so, then we might draw a horoscope of Germany and derive its tortured contradictions from its constellation of rivers.

Near the Danube, as it widens and flows horizontally, with little old houses mirrored motionlessly in its waters, rises Ulm Cathedral—tall, straight, soaring, solitary. This immense Gothic edifice and its larger and older sisters in Germany and France are, among the works created by the hand of man, those that most powerfully awaken the miraculous sense of imaginary and impossible things. They are like huge prehistoric trees (perhaps the Tree in the Garden of Eden?) born in a cultural desert; and one finds it hard to understand from what depths the inexhaustible saps necessary for their flowering have been drawn. They are entire worlds, unified in form and thrust, swarming with countless people, with cylindrical blocks, pillars, ribbings, statues, hidden figures, winding passages, orifices, spires, windows, lifelike persons carved in stone, hideous caricatures, allegories. They have the totality of mountains and ants—a totality that is at once synthesis and infinitely detailed analysis. They are Divine Comedies governed by secret numbers and symbolic relations, detached from earth yet abounding in the daily incidents of the medieval village, the customs of the craftsmen's guilds, the familiar everyday faces, and the monstrous spirits of night. But in these endless enumerations of an ancient reality we grow aware of another aspect of this miracle: these are extraordinary machines of the sky, forerunners of a later day, thrust into the future. They are gigantic machines, invented by prayer so many centuries before real machines—with the same cold, relentless impulse to soar skyward, at once mystical and rational, which in our own day has hurled new satellites toward the moon.

These gigantic machines of faith, products of the only big industry in the Middle Ages, stand isolated and apart from the earth. They tower over the tiny houses and are not to be compared with them. They alone have been freed from the sense of weight and the power of gravity, transmuted into a balance of tensions and forces; they are forests of stone, impelled solely by the plantlike impulse to rise higher, disembodied in the magic and orderly perfection of numbers. Here—and by here I mean in countries such as Germany, where no Renaissance brought things back to earth, to a feeling of solidity and harmony of the senses—is the starting point for the farthest-reaching, almost unimaginable roads: not only the basic elements of modern art and architecture but also, as indirect yet inevitable results, the Reformation, the Industrial Revolution, the triumph of technology, the splitting of the atom, and the flight into outer space.

And here, on the banks of the flowing rivers, beneath these isolated and magnificent forests of thought and stone, the spirit of totality lives in its natural house; here are born its legitimate and terrible children: dreams, ambitions, messianic hopes. "The whole country is in a state of expectation, and a low sky, weighing on us as in the hottest days of summer, covers us with shadows and premonitions, O nostalgic rivers! Full of promise, yet it seems to me to contain a threat. . . ." O Germany, child-priestess, rich in names, language, words, O thou powerless, thou disarmed, dispenser of counsel to kings and peoples! Beneath thy cathedrals poets and philosophers have invented great thoughts and missions, a new Greece and new gods. They have also invented the most frightful myths of the first fierce unity of the barbarians as well as the abstract and inhuman grandeur of universal suicide. But in our industrious—and so empty—years, not even dreams, either innocent or evil, rise up out of the silence. "The gold gushes more profusely than water from the springs; and the wrath of heaven intensifies." But now there is no one to look for "the truth between day and night" which Hölderlin dreamed of. Or if there is, he has not appeared; he is not heard.

Here in front of the church tower said to be the

tallest in the world, battered by a howling icy wind, I found it virtually impossible to pause and glance at the details: the figures facing one another on the foliage of the column heads, the winding staircases, the clusters of organ pipes, the pillars carved with twigs and knots, the host of saints, the exquisite filigree work in stone, the intricate web of vaults traced at the highest reaches. Biting, freezing blasts of wind made us scurry almost around the entire Cathedral. Minna shivered with cold in her lightweight overcoat. The wide bomb crater in front of the church façade was occupied by the wagons, tents, and booths of a fair; on the narrow old streets we caught glimpses of large draft horses plodding past. A fire was blazing on the pavement. Its sputtering yellowish flames were vaguely reflected against an angular medieval structure, the old salt depot, the most important building in Ulm after the church. Beneath the towering spire of the Cathedral, it would seem that the terrible and marvelous impulses that have been born here across the centuries, and that everywhere—even now—lead to the most unpredictable results, have left only ruins. The delusions of grandeur have turned into inferiority complexes; and around these ruins humiliated or alienated men turn as on a treadmill.

Next to the Cathedral we found a Spanish restaurant and went inside. While we ate and snuggled as close to the fire as we could to get warm, the proprietor chatted in his native Spanish with a dark-haired Mexican and a NATO official in uniform. (Incidentally, I believe this was the only NATO official I saw in all West Germany; he was a Puerto Rican of mixed birth, with dark skin and black liquid eyes.)

(V I I)

SPEEDING along the *Autobahn,* the superb highway project begun by slave labor under the Hitler regime, we passed more rolling hills and placid villages and dank, mysterious-looking forests, until at nightfall we were at the approaches to Stuttgart. The city, seen from the top of the wooded heights that dominate and surround it, sprawls out with its lights and factories over a wide area. It looked to us like a very big and attractive city. Once, of course, it was one of the most beautiful cities in Germany.

> Crowned with the sacred garland, the
>   illustrious city
> Already raises its radiant priestly head.

Marvelously it rises, bearing the thyrsus
  and the fir tree
Toward the happy purple clouds.
Be gracious to the guest and his son, O Queen
  of the mother region,
Blessed Stuttgart! Receive the stranger kindly!

But of all that nothing—or almost nothing—has remained. The hotel at which we stopped was the Graf Zeppelin, opposite the railroad station. It is new and the best in the city. On a little table in my room I found an invitation, in four languages, to visit the Mercedes-Benz factory at Untertürkheim and the automobile museum of the Daimler-Benz Company, *mit über 150 historischen Objekten* (containing more than 150 historical objects). I still recall with pleasure the unobstructed view of this industrial city— hard-working, smoke-filled, squalid—which I got from my high hotel window. I obtained an even better view, similar to that of a bird in flight, when I climbed to the top of the television tower which rises like slender tracery among the clouds. Here at this topmost point the winds from the heights whirl the snow violently against the windowpanes of the restaurant in the tower, which seems perched in mid-air.

But when I strolled through the brand-new streets

that evening, amid the heavy traffic and the brilliantly lit stores, I found nothing but temporary things, barracks-like buildings of metal and glass, showcases, copies of small-town American models. Everything was rich-looking and shiny and short-lived and monotonous. The structures, although unstable, fragile, temporary, and abstract, were not without a certain cleverness and intelligence. But they had no ties with the earth; they were without any true character and style. It was a bright and sparkling and transparent world, all façade, which seemed to have absolutely nothing within and behind it. The rebuilt City Hall, pride of the city, was a ponderous structure with a blunted tower, identical in design with the railroad station. We went down to the spacious halls in the basement, where there was a municipal restaurant. It was brilliantly lit and furnished with modern décor. The rooms had the solemn authenticity and respect for historical accuracy of a civic monument. Between the tables there were showcases exhibiting, in museum style, old curios and documents pertaining to the dishes, receptions, and festivities of ancient banquets—recipes, pewter, and menus of past centuries —taken from the city archives. It was not an inexpensive or popular restaurant. So I was unable to order a simple dish of *Knödel* (dumplings), which,

78

through some literary memory of childhood and with a tenacity that only increased as I went along, I vainly sought wherever I was in Germany. I told Rainer and Minna that the same thing had happened with regard to *kvass* and *kasha* when I had been in Soviet Russia. The obvious things are the most invisible: only poets and peasants see them. Rainer, who, after so many hazards of exile, loved his regained homeland as though it were a bedroom of his own, held forth at length on the excellence of German cooking and on German faithfulness. We walked through the nameless streets—so lacking in faithfulness. Gradually, as I looked at the selfsame flashiness and glut of merchandise in the heart of the city, I felt a deep sense of boredom and discomfort. I longed for an old wall or a serene face.

At the railroad station, my friends told me, there was a café open twenty-four hours a day that served *espresso* coffee. There was also an all-night movie and a bar, with the usual run of station occupants: people wanting to keep warm, those waiting for trains, and those doing nothing but just waiting. Rainer and Minna left me at the bar. It was late and Minna was tired. I was alone but still didn't want to return to the Graf Zeppelin Hotel across the street. On the stools next to mine I noticed two young men, dark-skinned and with black hair and eyes. Their faces had an olive-green cast, quite different from the usual faces here; and they bore a striking resemblance to Sicilian peasants. Perhaps because they had heard me speak French to Rainer, they addressed me in that language, taking it for granted that I was one of their kind. They were Algerians. They had come here from Paris, where they preferred not to be on account of the police.

"Here there's work for everybody. I'm a real good mechanic," the more talkative of the two asserted with naïve conceit, while his companion sat there and listened intently. "Why, I can assemble a car all by myself. But right now we're workin' in the building trades. How about you? You lookin' for work? What do you do?"

"I write," I answered somewhat timidly.

"Oh, you do lettering on signs. Say, that's a good job, you'll get good pay. You see, no one's out of work here and they pay pretty good. But I don't like the weather. I'm not goin' back to France, but I'd like to go somewhere else. Tell me, is there work in your country, in Italy? My mother was Italian; she came from Rome. She's dead now. But I have relatives in Rome, they run a café on the Via del Pantheon. I've never met them but they keep asking me to come to

Rome. They like me; they want me to go there. But I can't make up my mind—I'm afraid I'll never be able to go there. See what I mean? The only thing a man has is freedom. If I go to Rome I'm afraid I'll lose my freedom. My relatives won't ever want to let me leave there again. And then they say there are terrible things in Italy. I mean terrible beautiful things. Once you've seen them, you can't go away. Here, feel"—he took my hand and brought it to his chest—"I've got two hearts here. One heart tells me: go to Rome. The other heart tells me: don't go there."

A young German was attracted by our French. Blond, wearing eyeglasses, a beret, and a yellow raincoat, he intruded on this strange peasant poetry with a kind of oafish banality. *"Vous parlez français?"* he began. Then he continued, his face lighting up at the prospect of being able to practice this language he had learned: "French is beautiful. It's a language for women; Spanish is for men."

"And Italian?" I asked him.

"Italian is for singing. Now you tell me: How do you like German? What impression did it make on you the first time you heard it spoken?"

I told him I would answer by quoting an epigram of Goethe.

"Of Goethe and Schiller?" he inquired.

"No, of Goethe."

"Oh yes. Goethe and Schiller. Goethe and Schiller," he repeated, convinced that the two names must go together.

"Goethe and Schiller," I replied, resignedly linking the two, "Goethe and Schiller, if you wish, wrote an epigram that reads something like this: 'I have tried many things: drawn sketches, made engravings, painted in oils, modeled in clay—but, ever fickle, I have learned nothing and carried out nothing. Only one talent have I brought close to perfection: the most difficult thing with the most complicated instrument—writing in the German language.'" (I purposely altered the end of the epigram so as not to offend my German acquaintance. Goethe actually wrote: "That is why I, unhappy poet, work on the worst material—*in den schlechtesten Stoff*—art and life.")

The blond German gave no sign of understanding the quotation. "Goethe and Schiller, what greatness!"

"But," I timidly added, "if you could choose between the two, which one would you prefer?"

"I can't say. Goethe and Schiller."

"Which of the modern German writers do you like best?"

"To tell the truth," he replied, "I haven't time to read them. I'm an architect."

"And among the architects?"

"I wouldn't know. There are so many. I design houses for small families. I have my work; I don't have time to do anything else. Now there's peace. No more wars, never again! My brother's a doctor. I design houses for small families—and let's not talk about wars."

"Goethe and Schiller," I said as I bid him good-by.

(V I I I)

STUTTGART as I found it, after its destruction and reconstruction, with its past shattered and physically blotted out, had room only for work, and for men of work, in its machine shops, automotive and chemical industries, publishing houses, and magnificent printing plants. The street crowds, absorbed in their work, without any other outlets, were smug-looking, impervious to the "dangers" of culture, satisfied with a peace without problems or anguish. What eventually may emerge from this conformist emptiness is not apparent from any outward sign. Not only Stuttgart but all, or almost all, the old smaller cities of Germany are dead as far as their past is concerned. Gutted by bombs, they have been rebuilt and made unrecognizable, or cleverly faked. Few of them have not had to undergo this violent transformation. Rainer, who insisted that he felt good here, as in Cologne or Frankfurt or his home town of Düsseldorf, where he had his house and family and children, wanted to take me to see some of the rare spots that had remained. They were the places of a Germany which, to him, required a fresh start and in which now, after the romantic adventures and dramas of a long life, he was waiting with millions of others—for what? Perhaps nothing.

I think he found the search for these remnants of memory a bitter one. But how gentle was the country-side through which we drove the following morning. Once we passed the industrial suburbs, where there was one new factory after another in the modern style of architecture, we found ourselves in the heart of the old Swabian region. Here were quiet vistas, forests, towns, and villages that seemed to live intact—outside of time. We rode beneath a gray sky and in light rain along the road leading to Schwäbisch Hall, passing an orderly landscape of fields and woods that reminded me of the muted calm of certain Piedmont landscapes, but more tenuous and on a smaller scale. Side roads appeared and disappeared, winding up and down through the fields in familiar fashion, among trees arranged in a well-remembered pattern. Castles loomed on the top of hills. In the villages through which we passed, the inns and taverns displayed large signs in shiny metal bearing their names and symbols and pictures of the unicorn and other animals of heraldry. After rising for a long time in this rolling countryside, the road plunged unexpectedly and with sweeping curves into the heart of a dense forest. We went past trees on a carpet of pine needles mingled with water; we drove over old snow piled up in drifts by the wind and preserved in the shade. Through the thin drizzle, which was like a transparent, virtually colorless mist, a broad plain appeared below, as if at our feet. It was crisscrossed by rivers and brightened here and there by the timid rays of an invisible sun filtering through the gray clouds. We were at Schwäbisch Hall.

It is one of the few cities that have remained practically untouched; and its stones are the original ones, not imitations by well-meaning rebuilders. Its little world is that of a people who felt that here beneath the protective mountains they and their closely knit families would possess a permanent refuge despite the most fearful storms. We went over the old bridge spanning the Kocher River; we drove past the medieval houses overlooking the steady, crystal-clear waters of the stream's minor tributaries, crossed a covered bridge encased in a wooden framework, went past venerable walls, towers, heraldic arms, and houses with Gothic windows. Finally we mounted the top of the citadel, to the Romano-Gothic Church of St. Michael. The church square completely sums up the previous centuries. Flanking it are medieval houses with pointed turrets and the imposing Rathaus. The latter, multicolored but predominantly white, is a large boxlike structure, with door handles, rococo ornaments, and curves that bespeak craftsmanlike solidity and grace. Opposite, at the top of a very wide and high staircase, stands the church, preceded by its Romanesque tower. On the central column in front of the door is a stone statue of St. Michael, resembling a sweet young maiden who has awakened early in the morning and, still in her chemise, is sweeping the floor of her room with a sword. All around the church the ancient tombs, statues, bas-reliefs, and funeral inscriptions tell a story uninterrupted by death.

Inside are the famous wood carvings of the old Swabian masters. But first I spent a long time looking at the many sixteenth- and seventeenth-century votive paintings hanging all around the church. Some of them are on religious themes, folk-art imitations of

Italian mannerisms, with the figures disguised in Württemberg and Franconian dress and, beneath them, pious likenesses of the devout family making the offering. Often, however, the painting consists only of this scene: a family grouped around some religious symbol—a crucifix or Calvary—in a desolate landscape depicting the end of the world. The families are painted in a meticulous and accurate manner. But only the father or mother or some other important member, such as a first-born son, an uncle, or a grandfather, has the precise features of a portrait, with a realistic depiction of mustaches, beards, hairdresses, and medals. The children, with anonymous faces, looking all alike and wearing identical clothes, are lined up on both sides: on one side the sons, on the other the daughters, all of whom resemble tiny nuns. Those who were married at the time the picture was painted and thus had acquired the right to have a face, have their wife or husband next to them, with their children gathered at the sides. A tiny cross above the head of some of the youngsters indicates that they died in childhood. The stillborn, or those who died in earliest infancy, are, however, painted at the feet of the family group. These tiny bodies lying on the ground wrapped in swaddling clothes are like little white *Würstel*. Frequently, the

more clearly to indicate death, a red cross is painted
on the swaddling clothes; at times it forms the vague
outlines of a swastika.

These paintings, depicting all the best-known
families in the city, tell a complete story of the place.
Those mustachioed faces, those stern devout eyes,
those features stamped with bourgeois and religious
austerity, those rich notables surrounded by their
numerous, anonymous, and disciplined brood and by
their infant dead delineated with bureaucratic, affectionate detail, have seen and made and endured
the Reformation, the religious wars, the peasant wars,
the famines, massacres, epidemics, fires, and destruction, extending over two centuries; and here they
have written themselves down, beneath crude crosses,
in their best clothing, to show for all time their family
rank, their bourgeois dignity, and their untroubled
conscience. As true-to-life and conformist as they
are, complacent and pitiless, falsely secure and without imagination, those figures have the same sadistic
and domestic cruelty (O Mother Death, O Fräulein
Trude!) as some of the Grimm Brothers' fairy tales.
One would say they had been painted by some arm-
less artist—such as a certain Thomas Schweicker,
whom one sees in a fierce-looking portrait, patiently
illuminating initials with his feet. I went searching

through the city's bookstores, libraries, and archives to see if I could find a book about these pictures and these families. No one seems to have written about them—which is indeed strange in a land in which the most minute research has been done on the most useless and trifling subjects. A little digging into the archives and some systematic research, and a great deal of imagination, would give us an extraordinarily true story—or a really gruesome tale.

Next to St. Michael's Church, at the sign of the eagles, was the old Adler, an inn dating back to the 1500's. By the time we entered, it was late and the kitchen was closed, so we had to take potluck. But the waitress serving us bore a remarkable resemblance to a Gothic angel, like a figure from one of the cathedrals come to life. She had the same slightly slanted eyes, the long and sinewy neck, and the slightly rounded back. I told her so and she was shyly pleased. Unfortunately the proprietor had modernized the main dining hall of the inn. Even though it was still closed to the public, and painter's scaffolds were still up, he was eager to have us visit it. He was having the city's history painted on all four walls.

As we entered, the artist, an elderly professor from the local school of arts and crafts, was pedantically explaining the theme of his pictures to a sizable

group of students. The story began, of course, in prehistoric times; then came the Celts and the tales and
legends of the Middle Ages. But the most important
pictures were those concerning salt—the ancient salt
spring around which the city was born and the salt
mine that was later discovered and for many centuries thereafter became the chief reason for the
development, prosperity, and art of Schwäbisch Hall.
The professor's other source of inspiration was the
notorious evil spirit, the diabolical monster who for
centuries had roamed the surrounding countryside.
The artist then repeated to his listeners, in the very
same words, the logical analysis the inn proprietor
had given me a few minutes before: "Salt makes
thirst, thirst makes beer, beer dulls one's intelligence,
and this convinces one of the presence of evil spirits."
Thus salt has created cities, their beauty, their wealth,
their angels, and even their demons.

(I X)

NEXT MORNING we were on the road leading from Stuttgart to Tübingen, driving among dark pine forests. Rising on a low-lying hill was an old monastery surrounded by a tiny cluster of village houses with half-timbered architecture. The steep wavelike roofs were like meadows on a mountainside; or, in their diversity of colors, like age-old tapestries, the colors ranging from the muted pinks of the tiles to the greens, yellows, and violets of the mosses and the grays and blacks of the weather. Below were rooms, stables, open galleries, long interior staircases covered by ancient penthouses, muddy country roads, and the animal world of a peasant land. The view from above was a fleeting one—yet so compact, harmonious, full of peaceful silence, of rural freshness and intimacy!

A little beyond that point we ascended, through the great gates and stately courtyards, to the top of Tübingen Castle. Here, as everywhere around, schools of the University had been installed, amid the tombstones and memories of kings. And the vista which now unfolded—of the city, the river, the distant fields, and even the far-off horizon of the Black Forest—was made up of the same concentrated intimacy. But the expanse of roofs was a petrified sea of endless waves, delicately colored, achieving the most bizarre, pointed, and stirring architectural effects, a continuous variation of acute angles, like a many-hued, crystallized covering for dreams. Dreams of centuries stagnated beneath those roofs, in the narrow rooms and ancient alleyways where everything was intact, full of time and memory, that wonderful and natural endowment of children. (Only in these concentrated knots of memory do children everywhere flourish and expand. And so it was here too, on the cobblestones that resounded with the echo of countless steps.) Many children, a rare sight in that part of the country, followed us and stood around, playing games, leaping about, making faces.

Accompanying us was a journalist, a well-known

person in Tübingen. He knew more than any other resident of the city. He knew about everything: every stone, every window, every inscription, every artisan's shop, every sign. We descended quickly from the *Schloss* to the Town Hall Square, an enclosure with garlanded façades in which every house was the familiar and abbreviated story of a family down through the centuries; we passed the old inn and the Rathaus, decorated with portraits of the most renowned burgomasters as well as of Cotta, Uhland, and other personalities. The winding streets, the houses at different levels, the tortuous passageways, the sweep of the roofs, the diversity of colors—all gave the effect of a continuous spiral, as of a sea shell bringing to the ear the lost sound of the ocean of time.

Here was the college—called the *Stift*—at which for four years, between 1788 and 1793, three young men were students together. Their names were Hegel, Schelling, and Hölderlin. This courtyard was theirs; this fountain theirs. How young Germany was then, how young Europe was! "What gentle thoughts, what hopes, what choruses . . . So human life and fate Appeared to us then!" Here was the carpenter's tower where for thirty years the insane Hölderlin lived.

We passed the old University where Melanch-
thon once was rector. It was still part of the University but now housed the dental school. Once through
those venerable windows fanatical or enlightened
eyes gazed at the river and thoughts of theology and
philosophy came into being. Now we saw there white
smocks, mechanical molds, and formidable-looking
dentist's drills and lamps. We entered a medieval
house located on a secluded lane to visit the chamber
theater there. A young woman awaited us. She was
both director and actress. Graciously, smiling
sweetly, and with a profusion of animated gestures,
she showed me the stage set on which her children
were rehearsing for a performance. The medieval
house of the hatters' guild had a tremendous red hat
attached to it, almost as big as the building itself.
Other medieval houses huddled, like sheep around
their shepherd, close to the high, lovely, stately,
three-cornered mansion of the old salt depot. From
here ran the salt routes, along which communities
originated and prospered. At that time salt was a necessity of life, as precious as wheat and gold in a
closed world confined within narrow limits. These
commodities meant trade and were the first to batter
down the defenses of the castles and shatter the isolation of the cottages. Down the streets and over the

bridge the young Tübingen students swarmed in pairs and in groups—a youth that seemed preserved from the ravages of time.

Tired and hungry, we finally entered an old restaurant said to be famous for its excellent food. The waitress, tall and impeccable in an immaculately starched apron, greeted the journalist accompanying us with effusive warmth. She seemed to have recognized an old and long-lost friend. He explained to us that as a young man he used to eat here regularly but that this was the first time in twenty years he had entered it—ever since the day before he was married. Here, in accordance with a long-established custom, he had held a bachelor's dinner with his friends, thus marking the end of his unwedded state. After that one was not supposed to enter the place, since in that way it remained sacred to one's former life. If today, after so many years, he had come here, it was without thinking. He wanted to keep us company and have us taste the *Würstel* and the clear Württemberg wine. The waitress was the same one as twenty years before; even Argo, the restaurant dog, had recognized him despite his wrinkles and white hair.

Later I strolled by myself along the Neckar, in the direction of the setting sun. I sat down on the riverbank in front of old houses, locked and deserted, with vine trellises in their gardens and purple bunches of Concord grapes still hanging on the vines. Students emerged noisily from the lanes and then moved on. Then suddenly, unexpectedly, came a moment of absolute bliss, a moment of magical perfection in the clearly defined picture painted before my eyes. The magic spread over the azure and gold sky, in the clear gray clouds on high, over the elms and weeping willows bent over the still water, over the expanse of ancient houses of various hues, their windowpanes lit up by the last rays of the sun. The houses were pale, agitated, almost unreal, pierced with windows that looked like eyes, intricately arranged, violet-colored, shadowy, made of silver, copper, and dancing smoke, thronged with the infinite silence of the dead.

Already the gold was fading and the gray fusing with it. An unearthly spirit spread over the riverbank. I left the embankment, crossed the bridge, and went toward the broad avenue on the other shore. The shadows darkened; one by one, pale dim lights appeared in the windows. Not a voice, not a sound, was to be heard. Beyond the mirrorlike waters, next to Hölderlin's tower, the smoke of a fireplace rose dense and white from a ridged roof; and behind this smoke a golden light gleamed on a curved façade. I remained for a long time in this ancient silence. Other smokes merged with the shadows, other lights shone in the darkness, until the sky was completely dark and black night came.

(X)

THIS DESERT of busy, hard-working, painstaking, persistent men, their eyes so firmly riveted on the object of their labor, or on money, its equivalent and symbol, that they cannot look either to right or to left; almost heroic in their limitations, living in a city rebuilt without character or roots, amid buildings that seem ready to collapse out of annoyance at their own nondescript character and which no river could mirror with narcissistic pleasure—this city of Stuttgart, where I too lingered on one foot only, for business reasons, is but one of the many centers of the powerful new Germany, bound as if in a tightly woven network. It is not one of the biggest and perhaps not the most typical. It is usually said that the heart of Germany is further to the north, where, beyond the forests, the giant combines of heavy industry are located—the black-earth country of coal and steel, flaming blast furnaces, magnates and factory hands, wealth and masses of people. But even here in Stuttgart the common determination which one sees stubbornly imprinted on the face of every passer-by is expressed in work alone. The people do not stop to look at the gardens, the green hills, or the leafy forests. They look at factories, at the prosaic goods of stores, businesses, and industry.

The morning was rainy, the air dense with smoke. It was my last day in Stuttgart. I intended to leave the next day for Berlin; Rainer and Minna would go on to Düsseldorf, where their children expected them. After visiting a factory in the suburbs, I spent the rest of the morning in the huge printing plant of a publisher to whom I was supposed to deliver that very day an essay I had written about Italy. It was to be illustrated by a well-known and very able photographer, with whom I had discussed the project at some length. This was one of the biggest and most up-to-date printing plants in Germany. The technical director, going out of his way to be nice, escorted me through all the departments. With his finesse and reserve he seemed more like an Englishman than a

German—an effect due perhaps to the many years he had spent in exile in England. Judging from my experiences of the past few days, I felt that many more émigrés had been forced to flee Nazism than I had previously imagined. A great many of them —cripples, amputees, men who had lost an eye, paralytics, those with faces disfigured by burns— still preserved on their bodies the harrowing marks of war. Even the extremely competent technician who explained the work process and machines to me —a tall, lean, elegant-looking man—was lame. Under his guidance I followed every step in the ultramodern color-printing process, culminating in the immense twenty-unit rotary presses, which looked like spectacular engines for transatlantic travel. The designers, printers, and general workers, whether tracing models by hand, preparing inks, or watching over the automatic machines, all had the same large robust heads and steel-rimmed eyeglasses, the same sure gestures revealing the "know-how" of masters of their craft. They showed the same undivided attention, tautness of concentrated effort, intentness, and satisfaction with what their hands were doing—as if deaf and blind to anything else in the world.

I spent the rest of the day in my room at the Graf Zeppelin. I had to finish revising what I had written.

A whole afternoon of work was ahead of me. As the hours passed, I saw the landscape of rooftops deepen and darken, the cars glide silently along the highway in the distance, the color of the sky change, the lights go on even on the far-off girdle of hills. I wrote, crossed out, rewrote. Oh, this portrait of Italy as of a person, a woman "with her dark eyes, her mass of long blond hair the color of grain on slopes caressed by a sea breeze, her flanks smooth as the seashore, her gestures mysterious yet familiar, her smiles of love, and the purple shadow of her clouds, the hidden sorrow of her loneliness; and her very ancient youth, the roundness of her ripening breasts, her frivolous foolishness and very profound wisdom, her industrious leisure, her vital harmony, and her tears"— wasn't that perhaps too lyrical a portrait? I tossed the pages into the wastepaper basket. The sky outside, iron gray, induced thoughts of winter cold, withering ferocity, the weariness of weeping. Yet maybe there was also a beauty in this indifferent space, too bleak and at the same time too intimate, which extended all around me; the beauty of some place where a man could be alone even though he was in the thick of things with his mastery of technique; the beauty of that which could not be expressed in our words but still remained to be wrought, out of the

buzzing emptiness of activity. This emptiness, this
active and imageless peace, which I gazed upon from
my tall window, might attract or annoy or repel; it
could also disturb. I asked myself how Rainer could
end by settling down here. He had always chosen to
live, no matter what sacrifices it entailed, in a world
of thoughts and feelings, in a world so unlike this permanent one with its fixed habits and diligent, undis-
turbed routines. In his world the only important thing
had been change, hope, the future—even the sacrifice of one's life for that future. What was Rainer's
new fondness for his regained homeland, with which,
as I had once known him, he had nothing in common?
I recalled his speeches of those bygone days, when in
his own way he would even quote Tacitus to me:
"Without regard for men or for the gods, they do not
even feel the incentive of desire." Other men and
other countries had molded his life, had been his
homelands, the places where he had fought. The Paris
of the artistic revolutions, Republican Spain, Soviet
Russia, and so many other lands. . . . Elsewhere
too had been born that contentment with futile efforts, that ever recurring patience, the weariness
that comes with hard-earned freedom. Certainly, I
thought, idealistic reasons had not brought him back
to Germany; nor had it been any yielding to sin or

evil, for he had always, from the very outset, been on the other side of the fence. Nor, judging from the way in which he talked to me, was there any real forgiveness or pity in him. What then had brought him back? It was not only discouragement and personal disillusionment. There was, I felt, a common ground between Rainer and his native country, a common point which could be reached from opposite experiences: the denial of self, in order to save at least one's own soul by hiding it.

So I looked up from the little table at which I was correcting my pages and glanced out the window at an urban landscape where nothing was stable, ancient, shadowy, sure of itself—only glass, elementary forms, and weighty masses that simulated strength. Perhaps the moment of total alienation under Nazism had only been a fierce effort to lash out, in rage and fury, at the loss of self. In the sheets of paper before me, I spoke of another country, my own. I did not wish to make comparisons or to hold it up as an example. But I thought of the paradox of the basic security of the Italians. I believe one may truthfully say that the danger of loss of self is less in Italy than elsewhere. One's personality is not formed within vague and uncertain limits. It does not have the liquid and monstrous character of a temporary combination, but grows around a nucleus of its own in which the process of self-creation is scarcely reversible. And this is true even where, because of poverty and age-old domination, existence itself is a hazardous daily conquest. There too, nevertheless, the world of unified knowing and creative doing is revealed. It is the world of poetic reason.

But what was now happening in the deep recesses of German life was, it seemed to me, the opposite of Nazi activity and a natural reaction to it. In order not to feel the danger of the uneasy self and the anguish that goes with it, in the grip of an inner split weighing on them and keeping them in bondage, the Germans preferred silence or the roar of the machines in the practical world. Rainer too had shut himself up in the world of practical affairs, but for contrary reasons: the high cost of ideals, the burden of freedom. So he had found himself again in his unrecognizable country. He accepted and defended it even in little things, down to the slightest details of everyday life, symbols of a lost life. And here, desolately, he was at his ease.

It was evening. I had finished writing. The city shone in the darkness and Rainer was knocking at the door.

He had come to take me to a writer friend who expected us for dinner. The man lived in an isolated country house in the woods, about fifteen miles outside Stuttgart. After a wide sweep around the entire city we drove along country roads past deserted woods. We plunged into lonely darkness, among thick stands of pine and fir on the hills, and unexpected clearings, valleys, and isolated knolls. At the entrance of the house two enormous dogs, the biggest I had ever seen, awaited us. More like lions, they were of the rare Leonberg breed. Guarded by these formidable-looking animals, our host enjoyed the solitude of a house furnished with pictures, antique furniture, and rare objects. His lovely wife and daughter lived there with him. The rooms were full of curious things: ex-votos, statuary, prints. On a table was a spiral-shaped fossil shell found by our host's wife in the neighborhood. It was a network of intricate lines and innumerable incisions. Our host explained to us that these markings on the prehistoric shell were said to be the places on which the fairies set foot. They danced all around in an ever widening circle, and these tiny signs, these marks, were their footprints; as the fairies, gradually enlarging their circle, came to the edge of the stone and the end of their dance, they then turned into beautiful maidens.

The mistress of the house was a famous cook. Her goulash with cream, her pork *griban* with strong cheese and Rhine wine, and her raspberry brandy were delicious. The evening was spent in conversation on the most oddly assorted topics: learned anecdotes about animals, Goethe's hatred of them, and how in the end the great writer was defeated by a dog. It was a story that went all the way back to Pliny and King Croesus, continuing with the medieval knights, the queens of France, the German popular theater, the Court at Weimar, the king's actress-mistresses, and ending with Goethe's dismissal as director of the Weimar theater.

Our erudite host seemed tireless in his narration. He was a man of massive stature, advanced in years but still vigorous, full of vital energy, affable, and endowed with brilliant insights. He was a curious sort of scholar, fond of rare literary and historical items and the precious refinements of culture. Quick to grasp even the most transient and surface manifestations of taste, he had no conventional or academic prejudices. I would have liked to spend a great deal of time with him and the few friends who had joined us in this effervescent outpouring of words. But I had to leave these masters of the forests and fields and rich solitudes. I explained that I had to get up early to fly to

Berlin. To my amazement I realized that people spoke very little about Berlin; yet to many of them it remained an ideal, a symbol, an intellectual image of glory. In these days of tension the problem of Berlin would be especially acute. How would the fate of that isolated and divided city be decided? One of the guests, a pink-faced courtly old gentleman with long slender fingers, said lightly: "As far as I'm concerned, if the Soviets were to take all Germany, I wouldn't care too much. But Berlin, no. Let them take everything but leave us Berlin. How can we put Berlin—intelligent, wonderfully corrupt, witty, decadent Berlin—in their hands? Let them take the whole West, but leave us Berlin."

The huge dogs, quieted by their master's command, accompanied us to the garden gate. The moon appeared from behind the clouds, and as we drove rapidly through the forests, followed us in lone splendor over the intermingled shadows of the pines.

(X I)

LARGE yellow-and-black flags hung from the high flagpoles in front of the Stuttgart railway station. Yellow-and-black banners fluttered in the gray morning air, over the square crisscrossed by yellow-and-black streetcars. And the landscape spread beneath the plane bearing me to Berlin was yellow and black.

Rainer and Minna had gone with me from my hotel to the airport. From there they meant to continue directly with their journey in the car. Along with many others in the waiting room, they stayed until the flight take-off. As I went up the plane ramp I could see them, pathetic children of Middle Europe, waving warmly and excitedly to me, as though I were departing for some unknown place in another world. Again I left them, as I had left Rainer so many years before, to face alone and with uncertainty a future of complex problems and scant hopes—a precarious and unprotected future.

Their feelings were not unique. To all of those in the crowded airport, the departures and arrivals to and from the distant city had something that was different from other flights; some special emotion in the greetings, the embraces, and the hurried exchange of bits of information; a mysterious and imaginary and nerve-tingling content. But inside the plane I felt as if in a familiar streetcar: children, women, toys, packages, Christmas presents, and the calm atmosphere of everyday events.

The landscape was yellow and black. The fields were a greenish yellow, the forests dark green and purple. In the valleys between the dark forests the white mist covered the fissures in the earth. Toward the north, in the direction of the wind, the dark woods gave way on one side to a white circle of snow and frost. I glanced down at this faintly colored carpet with its villages, homes, smokes, and mists. Yesterday how many hostile eyes had looked down on this gentle landscape—with the cold blue stare of a man preparing to drop bombs? Looks of steel, as the execu-

tioners unloaded their answer into the very bosom
and deepest heart of the *gemütlich*. But now we were
flying within fleecy white clouds in some sort of abstract corridor, crossing other black planes as we
winged over an invisible landscape. We were above
the other Germany. Was it Leipzig perhaps? When
later the clouds dispersed and everything appeared
in bright sunlight and the sky turned blue, the northern country looked different: dark lands dotted with
fields, yellow patches of woods, a gray plain with unknown towns and villages; then a river, and beyond
the river moors, glades, wooded areas, and a boundless forest bisected by an arrow-straight highway;
then large lakes shaped in fantastic designs, and the
first houses, vast sections on the shores of the lakes,
streets and mansions, and a square field in the center
of the city, green, surrounded on all sides by old
houses. It was Tempelhof Airport. We were over
Berlin.

So we came down from the sky to land in the
heart of an immense city. We saw it suddenly from
its center, without passing through any suburbs, and
its wide avenues were full of people. My friend Wilhelm von K. had come to meet me. He was an old
Berliner who had but recently returned to Europe
and Berlin after twenty years outside Germany. Old

in years and looks, with subtle, refined features, he had clear eyes beneath his balding forehead. His manners were slightly affected, his clothes old-fashioned in their elegance, his words a complete mélange of ingenuous irony, wit, and skeptical sentimentality, with just a trace of a curious American boyish confidence like a lone red poppy in a field of stubble. The hotel he had chosen for me belonged to his old Berlin; it was small and elegantly furnished, in the rich residential quarter of Charlottenburg. In my room, quiet behind double doors, was a wide inlaid bed with a high canopy. How soft the German feathers were! Warm, infantile, maternal nests. The chest was a Dutch antique, inlaid like the bed, with five drawers. On the little night table there was a Nestlé's chocolate bar to sweeten repose. Next to it was a white card with a printed message wishing the guest a pleasant night and sound sleep. Beyond the double drapes of the windows was the garden of a small square, with black trees looming against the open sky. I went out on the streets with my new companion.

Full of tales and images of the "German miracle," of Germany's lavish and sumptuous overflow of wealth, I observed the sections around the Kantstrasse as far as the Kurfürstendamm. They gave me a sense of the decay of time and the brittleness of the past. Everywhere among the handsome imperial and aristocratic houses with their great halls and high marble staircases, among the mansions of the old ruling class of the capital with its indefinable air of decay, I saw nothing but ruins. Real, unmistakable ruins, with grass growing in the chinks of the crumbled walls, all covered with scribblings; and ruins used as temporary sites for offices and shops. Pausing before them, Wilhelm von K., who had been part of the world of theater and culture and wealth in the days of the Weimar Republic and who was a sad repository of memories and news items, told me the names of the former occupants, and what sort of men they had been and how much power and prestige they had had. He knew everything, in a heart-rending way, about every stone. This heap of rubble, with architraves and cornices of the elegant windows still remaining, had been the mansion of one of the biggest bankers. Now students and young girls in slacks dashed past it. Farther along, in the middle of the vast square and ringed about by flashy cars, was the large church built by Kaiser Wilhelm for the privileged worship of the rich. It was now reduced to a gigantic ruin. I was told it had been a horrible and pretentious example of neo-Gothic architecture. Now, charred, stripped of its skin and structure, it had as-

sumed the dramatic respectability of time. Somberly
it rose into the dry, brisk, invigorating air that made
the city and its ruins come alive. Here was where the
Kurfürstendamm began, most of it rebuilt, with new
buildings replacing the famous ones leveled by
bombs; with new hotels, new stores, new cafés, new
showcase windows, in a long row on both sides of the
avenues. It was one of the most famous spots in the
world. But, whether it was the hour or the company
or some intangible presence in the air, its new wealth
had something melancholy and funereal about it, as if
built on a void or on the bones of the dead.

My companion brought me to a restaurant. It
wasn't one of those he used to frequent with the intellectuals around 1930. "It's the best. Actually, it's
not a good restaurant. But the Berliners think it's
good," he said to me as we entered. Later we spent
the last daylight hours strolling along the Kurfürstendamm. The cafés followed one after another in suc-
cession, their fronts similar to those of the Paris
cafés. They had large picture windows, were heated
by stoves, and were crowded with smart-looking people whose faces, viewed through the windowpanes,
seemed spent. Pastry shops followed pastry shops.
One of them, well known, displayed on its walls photographs showing how the place had been wrecked

and set on fire during the Nazi terror. A tremendous crowd moved along the sidewalks, much less German in looks than the crowds in Bavaria and southern Germany. They had leaner bodies and sharper features —the population of a great capital. But everywhere, all around my guide, arose the sense of an old Berlin that was no more; replaced by an abstract, gaudy, and sad show window without life. The men of the former Berlin were all dead. My companion, with his outmoded intellectual graces, seemed and felt like a lone survivor after a plague. That day, he told me sadly, Ferdinand Brückner had died—he had been one of the last. Gleaming buildings of glass and steel were going up; the shopwindows were crammed with merchandise. They were all heroes; all of them were on display, bored protagonists. But where was the Berlin of German legend, the Berlin that, according to Heine, had discovered irony, that marvelous invention which changes stupidity into wisdom? Night fell, thousands of lights glowed, the people hurried to the stores beneath the Christmas trees; and some Italian friends came for me, to take me to the other side—to East Berlin.

We rode through what was once the richest and most fashionable section of the metropolis, the Tiergarten. It was now a weird landscape of black trees and stark ruins. Far off in the shadows, isolated in a dreary clearing, some newly finished tall buildings—looking like medieval towers of the present—caught our eye. One of them was a spacious white-concrete structure, in the shape of an overturned hat, with one wing constructed in a wavelike design. It was a recently built American hall for meetings and lectures. We passed the Siegessäule, or Victory Column, and continued in the darkness along the broad deserted avenue. To our right was an endless field of rubble; in the middle of it a modest pile of debris marked all that remains of Hitler's bunker. Beneath it his unfound body has become a part of the earth. On the left, searchlights flashed their beams on Soviet artillery pieces and tanks—it was the Red Army Monument. Right behind it were the massive ruins of the Reichstag building. Skeletons of statues of horses, high on the pinnacles, were silhouetted against the waning light of the early-evening sky. The iron framework of the shattered statues had been left up there like abstract bones, like infernal horses of a Death Triumphant. Suddenly we found ourselves at the Brandenburg Gate, the boundary line. . . .

After a brief stop to get a pink card, which anyone coming from the Eastern Zone must show when he leaves, we drove along what had been Unter den

Linden. The broad avenue was dark; on both sides
were tall buildings interspersed with mounds of fallen
debris and yawning empty spaces. Feeble yellowish
lights shone in the modest shopwindows. Few pedestrians were in evidence on the sidewalks as we passed
the austere buildings of the Party, of Humboldt
University, and the untouched ruins of what had been
Berlin Cathedral. At this point Unter den Linden
ended at the huge dark square in front of the church
and museum. To the right extended an immense level
area covered with countless booths. It was the *Weihnachtsmarkt*, the Christmas fair.

We crossed the tracks of a miniature train which,
covered with flags and posters, was chugging its way
around the whole fair with whistle tooting and bell
ringing. It was the little train of the Pioneers, the
Communist organization for younger children. Big
banners attached to the coaches proclaimed the tenth
anniversary of that organization. At the entrance to
the fairgrounds, the "white bears" awaited us. Erect
on their hind legs, they approached silently as the
photographer with them got ready to click his camera.
Everybody stopped for this initiation ceremony. The
bears, after obtaining the parents' permission,
soothed in their arms any children terrified by their
costumes. Later, photographs would document this

human-interest scene in East Berlin. The "bears" greeted us too and offered their paws. They were incredulous when we said we were Italians. "Italians are dark," they rejoined as they stuck out their heads in order to breathe a little of the crisp evening air. One bear was a tall blue-eyed youth, another a young girl. But beneath their pelts we could not see their souls.

We mingled with the happy crowds streaming into the fair. Outside were the grays and blacks of the deserted square and murky Unter den Linden; inside, a dazzling oasis of lights, with people in a holiday mood, and a vast maze of tents, booths, signs, stands, vendors, exhibits, games, and wheels. An enormous star-covered Christmas tree towered against the black background of the Cathedral ruins. As soon as we entered the fairgrounds we stopped to buy lottery tickets for fifty pfennigs. My ticket was a winning one. This was a cultural lottery and I was entitled to two books. From the bookshelves in Section C, I could choose among a three-volume history of Russian literature, some German translations of Gorki and Paustovski, some illustrated volumes on Czechoslovakia, a dictionary of everyday language and slang, and a good edition of Clausewitz's letters. I picked out the last two.

We threaded our way among the booths in the midst of a dense throng. On all sides were very young girls dressed in sweaters or cloth jackets and slacks. Their faces were flushed from the cold and the excitement of the occasion, and their eyes sparkled as they walked arm in arm with their escorts. They were factory girls or office girls, with country manners, their gestures uninhibitedly free, as if they were alone in this human maelstrom. The men came dressed in every conceivable kind of worker's outfit: peaked caps, jerseys, dark suits, boots. Everywhere there were uniforms, soldier's uniforms, uniforms of this or that police force, green uniforms. The wearers had military caps perched on their boyish heads and their faces were without even the first sign of a beard. They looked serious, as though engrossed in a game, as though these uniformed youths were fierce but make-believe, nonexistent policemen. Workers passed wearing the red armband of the *Volkspolizei* —the People's Police. Everywhere we saw educational displays, pavilions explaining Soviet achievements, exhibits of anti-Nazi writings and photographs, and heart-rending pictures of concentration camps, gallows, and instruments of torture. There were placards with political caricatures of Chancellor Adenauer and John Foster Dulles, and large posters with slogans and mottoes referring to the Berlin problem, some of them in rhymed verse: "West Berlin must become the center of friendly contacts between the two German States"; and "Berlin, the old German capital, belongs to the Germans"; and "Out with the foreign regime of West Berlin!" Two slogans that frequently recurred were: *"Amis Raus!"* ("Americans, get out!") and *"Wir haben Amis und Spione satt. Westberlin wird freie Stadt!"* ("We're fed up with Americans and spies. West Berlin must be a free city!").

In this blend of ancient folk festival and modern propaganda the crowd possessed something strange and hard to define. There was a curious light in the night air, an ephemeral brightness in the faces beneath the lights of the booths. The coarse-textured clothes and the sturdy farmer's shoes in yellow leather bore the imprint of another day and age. This shining island, in the midst of the great darkness of the city extending all around us and felt, from afar, like an unknown presence, seemed to be reflected in the faces, expressions, and gestures—like an isolated fragment of time.

I had just arrived in Berlin and hadn't really seen anything yet. My eyes and other senses were steeped in first impressions; I was aroused by colors and the intangible something inherent in things. Often these impressions arose from the most insignificant, indefinable objects and sensations. The subsequent days might change these initial images and even reverse some of them. But no doubt about it: at the moment I felt that these men, women, and children in their rough-and-ready clothing lacking any modern smartness had a more natural and agreeable manner, and one that was closely related to a profound national and popular tradition. Their visible appearance, in contrast to the sumptuous, cosmopolitan, and excessive modernity of West Berlin, harked back to a pristine condition of long ago. I was reminded of the gaunt figures we find in the paintings of the early German primitives and of the meticulous depiction of their crafts. Here was a return to costumes which perhaps no longer really existed. Moreover, there was a kind of special gladness in their faces. Did it come, I asked myself, from this return to a long-lost sense of communal living? Or perhaps from the feeling of security in the presence of so many different uniforms, a feeling of unchallengeable order based on these outward signs of authority? Might it not be this very alienation and renunciation, openly revealed rather than buried beneath the hollowness of wealth, that gladdened those faces? Or perhaps, on the other hand, the violent social change, the leap forward, which was at the same time a return to a distant past, had enabled them to forget more completely the recent past and had lessened all sense of blame.

"Don't forget," my friends told me, "this is a proletarian city." It really was; and what I saw of it had, and wanted to have, a thoroughly proletarian look— perhaps too much so. Just as West Berlin, with its wide new avenues and its rich and motley glut of commodities behind its dismal ruins, seemed a little overanxious to prove that it was a capitalist city. Here and there I sensed something excessive, something violent and unreal—a kind of exhibition, a show window more than a reality, a flaunting of security that rested on a great emptiness, as if the houses were built on the icy surface of a lake which the springtime sun could loosen and melt in a trice. And I felt that the contrasting things I had seen in my first look at the two Germanys sprang, albeit in contrary fashion, from the same entity—as though they were but two faces of the same coin, on one side a human face, on the other an eagle, both stamped by the same die.

Walking among thousands of faces that seemed lighted by oil lamps of a remote German era, we passed beyond the stalls and booths until we reached the Spree River, whose waters reflected the lights. Organ grinders stood at the corners of the bridge or leaned against its parapet. They had the haggard, bony, tragic faces of the minstrels of bygone days. A turn of the handle and the notes of their doleful ballads poured out into the night air.

Next we drove in the car for miles and miles through the streets of East Berlin. "Under the spot we're now passing," one of my friends informed me as we crossed a square, "there are twenty thousand human bodies, killed in a bombing attack." Yes, one felt the presence of the dead! Here they were not hidden beneath any "miracle." We finally arrived at an immense new street—wide, straight, uniform— flanked by enormous and heavy edifices which seemed rigorously academic and unimaginative replicas of Soviet construction of the last Stalinist period. It was Stalinallee, the Kurfürstendamm of East Berlin. On one side, in the midst of dismal-looking buildings, rose the lone monument to Stalin with its plethora of cornices, pinnacles, turrets, and ornate windows. We entered the nearby Varsavia Restaurant. It was on the street floor and was set up like the dining hall of a big factory. The men, in dark suits, sat at the tables engaged in serious discussion as they ate, and now and then rose and politely offered seats to their wives. A group of diners at a table near ours aroused our curiosity by their impeccable manners and the bureaucratic impassivity of their faces. They were, we were told, employees of a factory outside Berlin who had taken their wives out to dinner to celebrate some special occasion or other. A young woman paced up and down in the corridor, pausing in front of the mirror to admire her white fur-trimmed coat, of which she was quite proud. In the halls on the upper floor, reached by an imposing marble staircase, well-mannered couples stiffly danced familiar waltzes. In this orderliness I felt an act of will, an exaggerated or distorted echo, violent and lackluster, which, despite appearances, gave a picture altogether different from the one I had seen in the streets and houses of Moscow. It was a transplantation to another soil—conscientious, excessive, and indifferent. It was a Russia without azure sky, without angels, without its cold blue brilliance and its warm splendor.

As we left the Varsavia we were caught in a sudden downpour. To return to West Berlin, I took the elevated railway at Friedrichstrasse. There were four stations—a night run in the midst of ruins. I wondered what mysterious population might be nesting there in the shadows.

Near my hotel on one side of the square I saw an enormous cask protruding from the side of a house. Entering the cask through a little door made of rounded staves, I found myself in Pulle's, one of the many night clubs in West Berlin. Abstract paintings lined the walls; at the tables aging intellectuals and young students talked or yawned and looked bored. In front of the curved counter of the bar there were swings fastened to the ceiling by ropes. Swinging like a child amid this modern squalor, I drank my last cup of coffee. At the exit a young man working in the cloak room recognized me. He told me he was a painter and that he took turns here with some of his fellow painters to earn a living. He had painted in Italy, at Ponza; and he talked to me meekly, courteously, resignedly, of his abstract art.

In my hotel room the canopied bed awaited me. So did the feather quilt, the wishes for a sound night's sleep, and the Nestlé's chocolate bar on the night table.

(X I I)

IN THE DAYS that followed, all I did during the time I had left was to travel about Berlin—the two Berlins. I went from one side to the other several times daily, as though they were not two cities, quite distinct and very far from each other, but a single city without boundaries or barriers. Thinking back on those days, I now realize that what I did in effect was to go back and forth across an imaginary dividing line. Perhaps I was drawn by an unconscious will toward denial and inner destruction of the absurd, the untrue, the artificial, and the false. I went back and forth by car, subway, and elevated train and felt increasingly that these two fragments so hos-

tile and contrary, these two countries now separated
by a profound cleavage of basic differences in economic and political structure, in daily habits, mode of
life, feelings, attitudes toward problems and things—
a cleavage made even more pronounced by a different educational approach on the part of those in
power, by a different pattern of wills, characters, and
passions—that they were nevertheless bound together
and virtually identified in their opposition. It was the
same image reflected in two facing mirrors. And since
on each side the world that was being built—growing
more radically divergent from day to day—was following the same rule and order in its formation, even
though it proceeded from hostile and contradictory
premises, on both sides the same methods and the
same inner laws of development were revealed.

Each of the two half cities tended to carry to
the extreme the principles of the world that governed
it, inflating those principles to the utmost under what
it considered the searchlight of world attention. On
one side, individual liberty, abundance, wealth, modern taste, decadence, indifference, finesse, personal
inequality; on the other, ability, work, sacrifice,
equality, participation, the feeling of a collective
community. But Berliners in both zones, no matter
how much determination and tenacious courage they

displayed in striving for these counterpoised ideals and realities, did not really seem to believe and hold to them. It was as if in both camps the two roads now being traveled—moving farther apart with each passing day until the distance between them might appear unbridgeable—were nothing but a means of action. This was not felt to be something absolute and necessary, but was accepted at the hands of fate and external forces in the world as a means of temporarily filling a void which no force, no ideal, no spontaneous will to unity, was capable of filling. Once one accepted this direction or the other, once one set out on this road or the other and, in a kind of stoic and almost sporting spirit, faced up to the sacrifices it entailed, this very inner void, this lack of autonomy in making primary decisions, together with an almost mechanical pleasure in preventing any self-questioning or doubt or probing of conscience, stepped up one's pace. Consequently, the greater the achievements, the more lifeless they seemed.

The same basic alienation was revealed, in opposing fashion, in the two Berlins—pathetic sisters of inner bondage. They stood face to face and competed with each other in everything, but in different languages. Identical and yet dissimilar, they mirrored each other. What one did, the other did not do. If one

shone with bright lights, the other, with equal tenacity, wrapped itself in the gray mantle of hard
work. The one flaunted its wealth; the other equally
flaunted its poverty. The one sought to hide the recent past of death and inhumanity so as to deny it
and forget it and pretend that it never existed,
whereas the other preserved it and constantly recalled it as an instructive *memento mori.* The one
left the old individual alone in his wealth and in his
poverty; the other guided and leveled new masses
of human beings. The one theoretically left the individual mind free to judge for itself, and the mind
thus liberated curled up on itself and did not express
itself; the other constricted the mind, yet paradoxi-
cally it shone beneath the ashes. Everything was different in the two parts—streets, houses, public serv-
ices, governing bodies, museums, memories, theaters,
culture, economic life. Each of the two parts seemed
to have chosen what the other had forsaken. These bisected worlds looked at each other with turbid eyes.
Like actors, they took on the looks and desires of
those who wanted them to be opposed. They faced
each other like two champions of different cultures,
without any possible contact. But they were champions of the same mold. Whoever observed them
without their arbitrary and make-believe fierceness,

129

realized that in that very arbitrariness, in that fierceness, in that nonexistence, in that desperation, they were identical.

The morning was clear and bright. I left a pointless conversation with some businessmen at the breakfast table of my hotel and joined Wilhelm von K., who had come for me. We were going to the memorial service for the playwright Ferdinand Brückner, which was to be held in the Schiller Theater in West Berlin. Gathered there in the spacious orchestra was virtually all of the old intellectual Berlin—or what was left of it. Wilhelm introduced me around, as though pointing out the venerable statues in a museum. I met writers, critics, actors, journalists, men of culture. The ceremony was perfect. At the exact moment it was scheduled to begin, Brückner's widow entered veiled in black. The man who was to officiate bowed, kissed her hand, and escorted her to her seat. An unexpected desertlike stillness came over the gathering. The lights went out and in the darkness we heard the notes of a concerto played by invisible hands. It was the "Allegro Maestoso," in four voices, from Bach's *Art of the Fugue,* magnificently rendered by musicians concealed behind the closed curtain. As the final notes soared in the air, a large screen was lowered and on it appeared a huge, wraithlike portrait of the deceased writer. Then, superimposed on the dead man's face, were long sequences of still pictures of scenes from his comedies, with noted actors shown in their outstanding performances. The lights went on again and speakers followed one another on the podium. There were long commemorative speeches by professors, critics, and men of letters, with erudite analyses that kept harping on the other Germany as a kind of *idée fixe* or obsession. Thus Senator Tiburtius declared, with many digressions, that Brückner's greatness consisted in his having expressed the reality of the common man in his pure and absolute qualities as an individual, regardless of the social class to which he belonged. He ended with a quotation from Goethe and implicitly contrasted Brückner with Brecht. There were still many speeches to come. I wanted to leave, but one of my Italian friends sitting next to me whispered that such a move would be not only discourteous but also impossible. During such ceremonies, he went on to explain, it was customary for the exit doors to be locked. Before another speaker could begin I hastened to the door, turned the knob, and went out. My Italian neighbor, flabbergasted, followed me.

It was Sunday. A pale sun filtered through the gray-blue mist in the sky. The air was crisp and sharp amid the buildings, the rubble, the leafless trees on the avenues, and the orderly movement of the great metropolis of West Berlin. The Dahlem Museum was very far from the Schiller Theater. It was easy to reach by subway, but not so by car. My companion, bewildered by the labyrinth of new constructions and new vistas opening up on every hand, had difficulty finding the right street. None of the many passers-by to whom we turned could give us the proper directions—not even some smartly dressed girl students with books under their arms, briskly walking on the sidewalk. Eventually, after numerous twists and turns in a lovely section of gardens and villas, we crossed the bridge of the metropolitan railway and found arrows and street signs directing us to that splendid collection of masterpieces.

Even in its memories, its works of art, its museums, Berlin is divided. The two Berlins that face and mirror each other deny and yet complete each other. The famous Kaiser Friedrich Museum, Germany's greatest museum, was located in the eastern part of the city, in the heart of the destruction. Right after the battle of Berlin, the Americans took almost all its paintings and brought them to Dahlem. The

132

Russians sent to Moscow almost all its works of
sculpture and architecture. The very month I was
there the Soviets had returned to the Berlin museums
the high reliefs of the Altar of Pergamum, the portraits of El-Fayum, and the statues of antiquity. Almost everything had been sent back; the rest was on
the way. Priceless works of art handed back—this
had been the great cultural event of the year, solemnly celebrated in East Berlin. Dahlem had re-
tained the sculptured head of Queen Nefertete and
most of the remarkable figures and plaster casts from
the studio of the sculptor Thutmose. East Berlin had
regained many marvelous pieces of Egyptian sculpture, including the small statue of the nude Nefertete,
with her young girl's breasts and rounded belly and
her sturdy thighs. West Berlin had the Nefertete bust,
its features so modern, so contemporary, that they
seem to have anticipated by thousands of years what
a woman's face today reveals of her manner and soul.
It could be recognized from a distance from the large
crowd of museum-goers milling around and gazing at
it. Like "Mona Lisa" or Raphael's "Madonna," it is
one of the most famous images in the world, trans-
formed by time into a privileged figure, an idol of the
masses. Who can tell why? Perhaps because of the
mysterious attraction of a woman's smile.

I studied it over the backs of the admiring spectators. Near it were various effigies of Nefertete's husband, Ikhnaton, or Amenhotep IV, that "revolutionary" Pharaoh, a dissident and an innovator. With his long face, long chin, and long neck, the Pharaoh was perhaps even more subtle, refined, elegant, and decadent than his wife. Together, the two monarchs seemed like world-weary twins—with their mystery of the "reserved blood" of sibling incestuousness.

"Her face is so much like one of today! Can't you imagine her as a kind of founder or precursor? A female Karl Marx of the feminine revolution?" A voice at my side addressed me in a murmur. To my delight I recognized Martin, a German psychologist, who had been born in Italy and lived there for quite a while. I hadn't seen him in years. My companion, Wilhelm von K., who had resided for a long time in East Berlin, tolerated no paradoxes about the revolution and its sacred institutions. So he gave Martin a somewhat forbidding look. I knew Martin, with his face of a visionary, his gentle hazel-colored eyes, his complex mind, his Middle European culture—curiosity about ideas, zest for theories, philosophy, psychoanalysis, astrology, and intellectual play. But I didn't know that Martin was in love with the Queen. He really must have been, perhaps because she reminded him of a living person who had played an important part in his life. At any rate, with his predilection for allegories, antitheses, allusions, symbols, and mental short cuts, he began a typical speech that was obviously intended to support one of his pet theories.

"The feminine revolution! Only a genuine revolution succeeds in changing the way people look, their facial expressions, the light in their eyes, the charm of their smiles. Christianity appeared with new faces, or taught a new way of looking at them. If we go through the streets and compare the faces we see with our memory of them, we won't recognize persons any more. This queen comes from remote antiquity yet has a face of today. Believe me, it's not an isolated case; it's not an odd example of a similarity in style or sophisticated taste. It's something that anticipates in reality, as if prophetically, the universal change that for almost two centuries now has been shaping new faces throughout the whole world. This metamorphosis is everywhere so continuous, so imperceptible, and so diffused that we are not aware of it. But it is the result of the greatest revolution in history. Following the revolutions of the past, which abolished both ancient slavery and feudal serfdom, this revolution is abolishing female slavery. Can't you see that on Nefertete's face?"

No one could stop him now. I knew he would pursue his analysis to the very end. "The invention of machine-made fabrics was perhaps the first step, or the first opportunity for this upheaval, the newest and most important of our time. It meant the end of servitude for female labor in the home textile industry. It seems a little thing, but what consequences! Since modern industry has made the *lanam fecit* (wool weaving) useless and uneconomic, the *domo mansit* (staying at home), the harem, veil, seclusion, and bondage for women have likewise become socially absurd. This unexpected impetus toward liberation has undoubtedly destroyed some wonderful values. I regret it, and the women especially regret it. Because, to tell the truth, women, however much slaves, were never really so in everything. To the contrary, despite harsh social restrictions, they were very free because of their animal nature and their divine quality of procreation. Of course, this economic change has placed women in a fundamental crisis which is far from over: an unemployment crisis much more serious than that of the artisans in the first period of industrial capitalism. And doesn't it occur to you that this unemployment crisis has helped shape the direction of idealistic thought and romantic sentiment? That it has been the basis for projecting, in an imaginary and subjective world, a reality which no longer existed and still doesn't exist? The crisis in the feminine world is indeed far from being solved, even today. If you stay a while here in Germany, where there's a shortage of men, you'll realize that. How many sorrows, delusions, and tragedies, along with the vigorous pride and the victories! It is hard to achieve harmony freely, but certainly this crisis is changing the face of the world in a revolutionary way. It is breaking women's age-old habits, opening their eyes to things, heightening their consciousness, giving a new complexity to love and the family. The mere fact that a young girl in Calabria cuts her hair short or goes out on the streets alone is, within the limits of her world, a storming of the Bastille—and you know that better than I do. This movement, of course, doesn't affect women alone; it is bound to influence and modify, by reflex action, the acts and will of men, of all of us. If women free themselves, we are the 'second sex.' "

Then, in front of the mysterious, impassive face of Queen Nefertete, I told him how one day, about ten years before, a student had come to see me. He was from a village built on the site of ancient Babylon. He said to me: "I am a communist because of the women. In my country we are all that way for the same reason. We don't know women. We can't even see them. For us the only women's faces are those of our mother and of prostitutes. Women are hidden behind their impenetrable veil like an object of mystery, until their wedding night. We don't know the person who is to give birth to our children. Let's not talk about friendship; it can't exist. We're communists because, in our Moslem countries, it's the only way offered us to lift the veil that shuts out the reality of the other half of the world."

Martin turned to his Pharaoh Queen: "Here there is no veil. Look at her compact and fascinating firmness—like a prehistoric Greta Garbo! And so modern! She strikes us as modern above all because we see in her the will and drama of the process of liberation and humanization and discovery in the feminine revolution. At the same time, look how real she is. It is the hieratic reality of a Goddess-Queen. She is a Sibyl, a Manifesto!" At this my Italian friend smiled. What strange ancestors one can find for revolutions!

All the early German paintings have remained in West Berlin. One can lose oneself for hours among the great and even the lesser painters of the first two centuries of German art, discovering in them the origins of so many moods and manners that have been reborn or have burst forth anew in our time: not only expressionism, which leads straight back to the German primitive painters, but also surrealism and naturalist *verismo*. After leaving Martin to his goddess, we studied a great many of these paintings, admiring the way in which these various elements mingled and were juxtaposed without fusing. We paused in front of "Repose in Egypt," by Lucas Cranach the Elder. Here, rustling through the trees, was the leafy Gothic-Renaissance world, the religion of the primeval forest of Altdorfer. But the angel shaded by these trees—was it not a painstakingly realistic portrait of the wife of the jurist Johan Reuss as she looked when young? I could have spent hours not only looking at these early German masterpieces but also making discoveries bearing on today. Here for the first time were revealed the problems of the cleavage in modern civilization.

As we moved through the halls, the transition to the great Flemish works of art was already a leap. The perfect Gothic, the unreal and eternal light, in Van Eyck's little "Madonna in Church" mirrored a different unity. This unity developed and changed in the works of so many others, finally opening out into a turbulent multiplicity. How much there is in a Rubens landscape! Tree trunks, cows standing open-eyed in the shade, rain falling from a cloud, hunters firing their guns, blossoming trees, swollen teats, houses hidden in the woods, far-off rivers, paths, peasants' carts, a rainbow, and the red sky seen through the branches. (In Rembrandt the many-sided infinite gleams with an inner light of consciousness: here we are already in the future.)

But then we left the rooms of the German painters and went down a short flight of stairs to the other side. Suddenly we came upon Titian's "Venus with the Organist." I was forced to make an even greater and more radical leap. I found myself passing a long line of masterpieces belonging to a world of almost incredible, absolute unity, a world in which beauty existed as an image of the perfect harmony between man and the world. At the end of this row I came to a painting by Giotto, and it struck me that he was the one responsible for that miraculous, and perhaps illicit, development of history and taste which for several centuries had held back the explosion of individual feelings and idolatries. Close to the exit we saw a series of paintings by Watteau and the impressionists, lined up like the last squadrons of resistance; and then the last smiling queen, Renoir's "Young

Girl in Summer," with the most delicate shades of green behind her black hair.

The hours passed swiftly. Outside, I barely had time to eat in the first eating place I came to. Hurriedly and without sitting down, I ordered two sausages with mustard and potato salad, which is often taken instead of bread. The two sausages, a white one and a red one, sizzled and smoked on the platter. Toward evening I was expected at a reception, but first I wanted to make a quick trip to East Berlin. How many times, in a few days, had I taken this ride in the elevated! The sun was shining that day and the dismal landscape of the denuded zone between the two cities was clearly revealed as a maze of ruins, lonely streets, dead and abandoned things, hiding places, refuges, and possible traps—like an abstract page of the remnants of history which no one had taken the trouble to rearrange and in the midst of which, here and there, splendid buildings arose, isolated and absurd. The industry of death and suicide had created these gray objects with the same random accuracy with which an unconventional artist composes his paintings. Nature made up of debased and humiliated human things as well as the natural landscape itself seemed to have the same anguished cleverness, the same lure of stickiness, dirtiness, and distortion, the same lack of innocence of those paintings.

A tremendous crowd, in a holiday mood, milled about anonymously in the *Weihnachtsmarkt*. It was altogether different from the feudal, nighttime crowd I had seen the day before. So different that I wondered whether I had been dreaming then. Now perhaps, on a sunny Sunday, the two Berlins had made an appointment to meet here and were mingling. The reserved character of old, medieval peasant Germany was diluted and lost in the flood of visitors from the West: students, young people, middle-class families, relatives who lived apart in the two zones and came together again among the fair booths. But the bears, the camera-conscious and the heraldic ones, were the same; and the old hand organs, the Italian name of their manufacturer written on them in Gothic letters, gave to the incessant sound of footsteps the remote quality and steady, desperate rhythm of an oft-told tale.

The holiday afternoon changed too quickly into nightfall. Countless lights gleamed on the crowded streets of West Berlin beneath the now darkened sky.

Streams of people flowed constantly past one another at the traffic lights, in front of the showcases, movie houses, and building façades, around the Christmas trees, beneath the sparkling stars. They walked in a brightness that hid the rubble—amid the shiny cars, beneath the girders of the elevated railway, past the stately old bank buildings and the sites of new wealth.

I let myself be carried along by these nameless, countless waves, borne here and there at random over the swarming sidewalks, until I realized I must hurry if I wanted to arrive at the reception on time. There I found intellectuals, journalists, and critics: Germans, Englishmen, Americans. Many of the foreigners present were keen observers. I also found veteran Berliners seasoned by the experiences peculiar to the "closed" years immediately after World War II. Many had not crossed the nonexistent boundary line for months or years, and they were curious to hear my impressions. Almost all of them recalled, with a kind of nostalgia, the time of the Berlin blockade. They spoke of the amazing technological feat of the airlift by which such a vast and populous city had been supplied for months, using only the small Tempelhof airfield, so closely surrounded by houses. They told of the restrictions of those years, of the fears, of the exciting and highly charged atmosphere in which they had lived solely from moment to moment. Now, they asserted, the Berliners were used to alarms, to heroism, to the ever increasing wealth; and they were also bored by them, indifferent to them. The present tension no longer fired their spirits. It was a repetition. They felt that it concerned others; that others could incite it, invent, worsen, or solve it. They didn't really believe in it; and, without believing in it, they were ready for whatever might happen. As a pretty and very elegant lady with deep blue eyes said to me: "We Berliners are all tired of playing the hero."

Reluctantly I had to leave my tired heroine. I had a dinner engagement at the brand-new Hilton Hotel. Opened during those very days, the Berlin-Hilton was the last word in newness. It was said to have cost well over six million dollars. The sum had been ostentatiously invested in that dangerously exposed frontier as much, perhaps, for psychological reasons as for financial ones. On both sides of the entrance, crowds of curious spectators had gathered as if to watch a reception of royalty. When the cars pulled up, the gods and semi-gods emerged and entered the Olympian precincts of the hotel. I was to dine that evening with several financiers accompanied by their

private Rosemaries. The floor in the new grand dining room was made of costly leather. The waiter
called my attention to that fact, which I would not
otherwise have noticed, for in color the leather resembled ordinary wood. But he added that the management had already had to change a few pieces,
because whenever something spilled or was overturned, the stain remained. Frankly, the dinner was
rather modest for such ostentation.

After dinner we said good-by to the magnates
and their Rosemaries. Wilhelm von K. wanted to
take me on a guided tour of the night clubs. The pro-
gram in all of them was fairly routine: women, satiri-
cal skits, and strip-tease acts. They were all over-
crowded and dull, even the one in which a beautiful
girl twirled her body within a hula hoop attached to
the ceiling by invisible nylon threads. The last one
we visited was a place frequented by artists and run
by a jovial Negro. There were pictures by Hofer and
other good painters on the walls. To escape from
these noisy, boring, dismally luxurious night spots,
we sought refuge in a popular bar on the Kurfürstendamm. The only seats we could find were at a table already occupied by two middle-aged women: a stout
blonde with eyeglasses and a little hat, and a thin
woman with a weary face who was wearing a thread-

bare sweater. Both of them were sitting dolefully in front of empty glasses. Behind us, standing alone, was a young woman with fine features and rings under her eyes. She was leaning against a beam eating a single sausage. We invited all three to a round of beer but suddenly realized that they might have preferred to have us order something to eat. They told us that this was a very good tavern and that they served really delicious pâtés. The big thick slices of pâté came up and *Würstel* were brought. The three famished women, affecting the very best table manners, consumed them with gusto in no time. Johanna, the fat one with glasses who looked like a schoolteacher, told us she didn't want to live in East Berlin: "Because in the East you can't *work*." Annie, the young one with the delicate sad features and light hair, told us that she was born over there in the East and that her mother was still living there. Once she had gone across to spend a few days with her. But she had waited too long in getting her papers stamped, so the police had come to the house and taken her to headquarters. In her handbag they had found many snapshots of Americans in uniform, her boy friends. The authorities had asked her, as the price of freedom, to work for them. She had said yes ("With them you have no choice"), but during the night she had escaped. That is why she had no desire to go back to the other side. The third one, Gertie, who looked like a former charwoman, visited East Berlin now and then. She had relatives there but didn't like it. "Over there," she said, "people seem different. All tied down, restricted. And there's no work."

Wilhelm von K. pretended—who knows why?—that we were members of a very important American mission studying life in Berlin. He said we had just come from the Hilton Hotel. The eyes of the three women shone. "The Hilton!" they exclaimed in unison, open-mouthed in legendary admiration. And so we left them, mouths gaping, in front of another slice of pâté.

(X I I I)

ALL the museums in West Germany were closed on Mondays. For some reason I had the notion that in East Germany they did not follow the same rule. So at noon I was at the entrance gate of the museum of the Pergamum Altar. I passed the columns and the courtyard with its staircase of honor and the symbolic statues that had survived the bombings. Beyond the gate was a sentry box, in reality just a wooden shack. A woman employee in a worker's jacket sat behind the ticket window, passing the time knitting. She motioned to us to stop. Here too the museums were closed on Mondays. Closed, that is, to the public; the doors were wide open and there was a constant coming and going of trucks bringing boxes, helpers unloading them, and officials superintending the work and then going inside.

On the boxes were letters in the Cyrillic alphabet, which indicated that they came from Moscow. They contained the last works of art brought back to Berlin by the Soviet authorities. A journalist with me, a person of some authority here, explained that I had to leave the next day. He asked whether, as a mark of special favor, I might be allowed to take a very quick look at the museum even though it was officially closed. The woman employee was undecided. She thought about it, made us wait, then decided to put in a few telephone calls. We remained for quite some time in the crisp wintry wind until at length a director came up behind a truck that had passed through the gates. The employee beckoned to us to speak to him. He promised to send us an assistant who would help us. A half hour passed, and still no one appeared. The employee, after several more phone calls, told us that the assistant was having her lunch and that we should just patiently wait for her. Finally, we saw an old man coming toward us from the door; he was tall and venerable and had two artificial hands made of leather.

He was a museum specialist, and he took us on a rapid tour of the halls. It was a real journey among the oldest splendors of civilization. The returned Altar of Pergamum and the market place of Miletus were perfect settings. The statues of the frieze, set up in a temporary place, irradiated their complex power and shut out time. The archaic magic of the most ancient gods of Egypt and Greece enveloped us; and we felt this all the more intensely as we hastily passed them without being able to linger. Then, all at once, we were on a great avenue between high walls of blue majolica, among figures of lions; and once again the world was different. Time had changed and had closed in around us: it was the Triumphal Way of Babylon. But the old man with the artificial hands made us move on. Soon, amid the clatter of the boxes arriving from Moscow, we had to leave. The pale sun awaited us on Unter den Linden, the Triumphal Way of ruins. How time shrinks, like a burning leaf!

Now we rode in a wide sweep across West Berlin. Two lovely ladies were with me: a Berlin painter and a younger woman. The latter said to me: "My city no longer exists. It used to be called Königsberg. But not only doesn't it have its name any more, there's nothing left of it except the harbor and a few waterfront offices. There's not even a memory of it—

neither Kant and his clock, nor the ancient streets,
nor the castle. There's nothing left."

We were on an immense plain that ended with a
railroad line. Here the international exhibition of
architecture had been held the previous year. Buildings by some of the most famous architects in the
world remained standing and were now occupied.
Some were beautiful in themselves, but in the emptiness which surrounded them they seemed unnatural
acts of will. We passed through the shattered Moabit
district. The name remained with me, a vague but
persistent memory. Suddenly I saw it before me,
quite clearly and distinctly: the Berlin prison. From
there we went to Wedding: interminable, depressing
rows of working-class streets. We skirted branches of
a river, passing one factory building after another.
On top of the tallest cranes were Christmas trees.

We passed through the populous streets of Tegel.
Then, entering a garden, we arrived at a large country house, a noted example of German architecture of
the early nineteenth century. It was the Humboldt
house. In East Berlin, in front of the university bearing their name, the two Humboldt brothers solemnly
sat in the form of marble statues. Here, behind the
house, a park unexpectedly opened out. The sounds
of the city, shut out by the park's magnificent green-

ery, did not reach it. Here, as far as the eye could see, was an avenue of very high trees bordered by a vast meadow; beyond it, in the distance, was another solid wall of hedges. We walked for a long time over dead leaves, unable to see any end to the straight avenue veiled by a light mist. The sky, through the branches, was like certain very light eyes one sometimes encounters. One cannot decide whether they are blue or gray, and they don't seem to have a true color but only an inner and phosphorescent idea of color—the unreal, German look of the eyes of my woman companion.

We finally came to the end of the avenue, the tomb of the Humboldts. All the members of that great family were buried here—twenty-three stones, all alike, arranged like a battalion of soldiers. Then we returned to the far-off villa, enclosed in this separate eighteenth-century, early romantic world of trees and lawns. The city was invisible and seemed nonexistent; the present did not reach here. Imagination whispered to us: How wonderful, how exhilarating to have been here at the start of the century, in the first hours of dawn, in the first years of youth, astride a spirited young horse and racing over the first grass! But, alas, this magic was not for us. We were not at the start of the century nor on a horse at early morn.

Nor did we any longer have the youthful green of the grass.

Outside, the city caught us up. Factory districts, monotonous houses, and a huge lake over which the shadows of evening fell. Then the dazzling lights of the huge factories of Siemenstadt, houses and buildings and streets and avenues, until we reached old Charlottenburg, the Zoo, and the elevated station from which I could return to the other side.

My friends were not at our usual meeting place in front of the *Weihnachtsmarkt*, so I waited for them in the company of the "bears." Observing me jot down some notes in my notebook, one of the "bears" asked: "Are you going to write a book? Will you tell about us too?" Maybe that was all I would tell about. My friends soon arrived and we went off to the theater of the Berliner Ensemble, which we had decided to attend. That evening they gave *The Good Woman of Szechwan*. It was a magnificent interpretation. Brecht's theater is certainly the most truly poetic thing left in Germany. It is just as timely and alive as in the days when its creator was living and writing. How closely linked this theater is to the earth, how deeply rooted in it! How far it goes beyond the bleakness and distortions of expressionism! It is indeed, as it is defined, an epic theater. The individual is never expendable. He does not act in accordance with reason, psychology, accident, or his own feelings; he acts solely in his inexorable relations with the world. He cannot change himself unless he changes the world. Yet his moral resolution is full-bodied and virile, not despairing. It is full of a bitter élan; it is the epic of revolution. "Can there be another man, or another world? Can there be other gods? Or no God?" The gods of Szechwan, in their gilded rags, aware of our forlornness, disappear into heaven. What's left in the world, unless it changes?

At the end of the play an actor came out in his epic tatters and addressed the honorable audience: What end can there be that is less bitter than the one ordained by the present, except in man's changing himself? Each one of us must look for it; and it must be good. *"Es muss ein guter da sein, muss, muss, muss!"*

(X I V)

AFTER innumerable comings and goings, my last evening was finally at hand. I had seen the various hours make each day a change of seasons, a change of colors, odors, and atmospheric densities. I had watched the population of the streets change every few hours. I had seen workers' faces and middle-class faces—and already, in so short a time, so many had I seen that for me the features began to lose their sharp contrasts. Already I was beginning to feel as if I were in a familiar room. I learned to distinguish places from the sound of a train speeding over a bridge, from the area of sky revealed by a distant light. But, just as a windmill whirling its black-and-white vanes seems uniformly gray, so my constant crossings between the two Berlins, although they showed me more and more the deep-seated differences between the two sections, ended by giving me an image of a single color. The rainbow of hours, places, contrasts, customs, and feelings gradually lost its many-hued texture and appeared to me at times like a great arc of blackness—uniform and nocturnal. The millions of human beings living on this artificial double island as if on an experimental reservation all prove that if, on the one hand, a different set of conditions quickly and profoundly alters the very way people look, nevertheless certain elementary traits remain immutable, like the quality of a voice that does not change with the years.

Here in Berlin, perhaps more than anywhere else in the world, all problems were posed, by the nature of things, with unusual violence. It should have meant that at every moment everyone had to make a choice, and from this should have arisen a dramatic ferment of life, ideas, and consciousness. But a force that was just as great impelled the Berliners to evade these problems, to shut them out of their consciousness by transforming them into abstract ideologies or daily routines, or mere gestures and attitudes—as if this were some accidental, make-believe center and only elsewhere were things real and alive. One could imagine powerful underground forces concealed in the shadow of the lack of self-rule. But in the history-filled streets I saw the women doing their marketing, the workers trudging silently to work, the wealthy passing in their flashy cars. The old Berliners waxed ironical in their nostalgia.

Toward evening, after saying good-by to Wilhelm von K., I passed through the gates between the two cities for the last time. In the ravaged Pergamum museum I moved about in the feeble light of an exposed bulb without being able to get at the heart of that inexhaustible collection. The portraits of El-Fayum have the magic of absolute truth, beyond art and expression—a truth that endures after the lapse of centuries and remains alive today. Here are eyes that look at you and shine, thoughts that are our thoughts, sentiments that are eternally alike.

In vain I hunted about in the maze of rooms for the friends whom I had vaguely promised to meet here. They were looking for me too. But as we climbed up and down stairs, moving among the Athenian and Roman queens and the birds of the Nile, the Greek gods and slaves, the T'ang horses, the architectural sculptures of Laurana, and the German paintings of the nineteenth century, passing and repassing the same spots, our paths did not once cross. As I left the museum, I assumed that they were at our usual rendezvous in front of the *Weihnachtsmarkt*.

It was a little after nine. The entrance to the fair was deserted; the fair itself was closed. The guards in their long tight-fitting military coats, their beardless faces impassive beneath their military caps, were drawing the barriers in front of the entrance. The square was dark, cold, and lonely. While waiting I paced slowly back and forth, copying on the cover of the catalogue of the art works returned by the Soviets the text of propaganda slogans referring to West Berlin that were painted on large placards outside the fairgrounds. Within a few minutes the guards grew suspicious of my leisurely stroll. One of them came over and, in a brusque, harsh manner, asked me about the book I had in my hand. *"Katalog,"* I replied, and showed it to him. When he saw it was a book on art, and a Soviet book, he softened to the point of setting out to find a taxi for me in the darkness. Not one of those passing through the dark empty square was free. At length I saw the guard rush toward one that was slowing down. He stopped it and proudly motioned to me. The passengers getting out were my friends, who had come to get me. The cab was a black de luxe Opel; seated at the

158

wheel was an elderly lady, formerly the owner of the
car and perhaps even of a castle or two. Now, with no
overt complaints and perhaps even with some un-
anticipated pleasure, she was earning her livelihood
as a cab driver.

We rode all around in the taxi as far as the out-
lying suburbs. The prosaic night of the working-class
city was full of alleyways, shadows, conscientious
hard work, austerity, and stubborn faith in a different world. These were my last looks and visits, my
good-bys before leaving. My friends, in their homes,
insisted on preparing for me some *cappelletti* they
had received from Bologna for the following Christmas. They opened cans of salmon from the Volga and
canned fish from the Baltic; they offered me Soviet
caviar—and oranges. This year had been a very
auspicious one. There were oranges for everybody,
vitamins, *Sudfrüchte*—fruits of the South. They had
all been able to fill their shopping baskets with
oranges and lemons at the *Weihnachtsmarkt*. Sweet
is the savor of difficult things!

Together we drove in the night over old and new
streets, passing the Writers' Club and the Budapest
Restaurant, where solemn-faced employees were
dancing an old-fashioned polka. We stopped to admire the small garden apartments for workers in the

new model district of Kleine Andreasstrasse, with tiny, carefully tended gardens that were the pride and joy of the tenants. We climbed the stairs to artist's studios that looked like abandoned factories, and as we went along we carried on a hurried conversation and fired questions at each other. What about the new Marxist theoreticians? What were the new writers doing? What would happen to Berlin, indifferent victim and detached protagonist of a game played by outsiders? It was like a city whose sky was crisscrossed by shells fired by two opposing armies encamped at its gates, its inhabitants sleeping through the uneasy nights in the most hidden rooms. Yet they remained alive and grew accustomed to the din. What was hidden in the inaccessible hearts of the bureaucrats, those shrewd administrators of the absurd, diligent systematizers and defenders of the division, rational guardians of madness? How would it end, this temporary tale of emptiness and cleavage between men?

These gloomy streets of ruins to which we came at about three in the morning, near the Brandenburg Gate, had once been the center of Berlin's affluence, elegance, and politics. Now one couldn't even make out their outlines. Beyond a line of barbed wire, in the no man's land, there loomed the vague contours of what remained of Hitler's bunker. To our left was a once stately mansion, now a jumble of debris, its walls cracked and jagged. I was told that this heap of bricks and dust had been Goering's palatial house. Curious, I entered through a gaping hole in the wall, taking care not to stumble over the beams and rubble. I found myself in the sordid obscurity of what remained of this seat of power and futile grandeur. My friends and their wives had remained outside in the car, waiting for me. As I was alone at last, and the women couldn't see me, without thinking twice I took advantage of my momentary isolation to urinate in the darkness against the wall. It was an automatic gesture, altogether unintentional. But suddenly, at the same moment, I realized that it was the very gesture Charlie Chaplin would have made, deliberately and with unerring creative intuition. It was not I in the shadows; it was Charlie Chaplin, who had come to the end of the movie, to the end of his adventures. Now, in the Dictator's room, he was totally free—freed from the slavemaster, freed from the head of the other world. Yes, there was an ending: it was Brecht's ending, and Chaplin's. That was what my involuntary gesture showed on its own. And it was a good ending because it was a possible one. Everything was finished; but, in this emptiness, a new day and age could begin. In the world—a world that is already so different—there was still hope.

(X V)

FOR THE last time we passed the Brandenburg Gate, the guns on the tanks of the monument to the Red Army, the dark waste of the Tiergarten. We drank a final cup of coffee at the swing in front of the bar in Pulle's night club. Then I returned to the very soft bed in my hotel room and, bathed in a vague sense of hope and friendship, fell asleep for a few hours before dawn and my departure. When the alarm clock aroused me abruptly and I got up from the last downy feathers of Berlin, from that nest of pillows and feather quilts which had the soft warmth of a mother bird, the gray light of earliest dawn was barely visible beyond the transparent curtains. I was trying to retain a dream I was having. I was entwined

in the dream as if in an endless ball of thread, and it
seemed to me that that skein had to be completely
unraveled so I could reach an important and secret
point that kept moving farther and farther away from
me. . . .

First I was in my room. I knew before anyone
else that in Spain, before long, there would be sweeping reforms. All those who could prove that they
descended directly from the kings—not more than a
thousand persons in all—would receive a million
dollars in gold and power corresponding to this great
wealth; the others would get money and power in
proportion to the antiquity of their lineage. In my
dream I said to a woman friend: "You have so many
ancestors and you're so fond of sudden impulses—
become a Spanish citizen right away. But be careful:
it seems that Jews and poets, except perhaps for a
favored few, are ineligible for the game." At this
point Spain disappeared. I was shut in on every side
by an endless flock; I felt the warmth of these animal
bodies surrounding me and pressing against me. I
was swimming rather than walking in the midst of
this milling multitude. I was in a vast green valley
ringed by very high mountains; it was an immense
lawn of soft, symmetrically trimmed grass. The
meadow was completely covered by the flock: mil-

lions of sheep, all alike, all of the same color, all equally gentle, were grazing together with heads lowered toward the earth. All of them had the same rounded woolly backs, the same stubborn patience in feeding. In whatever direction I turned I saw the same sight, the same extremely slow movements of these peaceful animals, like a field of wheat gently waving in the wind. Yet, even though no one showed me, I knew—with the irrational certainty of dreams —that there were two flocks. They were divided and separated in some unseen way, but in such a manner that they could not mingle. Tossing about in this dense throng of rumps and flanks, I finally found some faceless shepherds sitting in the shade of a tree in the middle of the meadow. Hanging from strings around their necks were reed flutes. But they weren't really reed flutes; they were gleaming trumpets. The shepherds held staffs in their hands. But they weren't really staffs; they were oddly shaped iron bars. Every now and then one of them sounded his trumpet. Then you could see the dogs come running up to keep the two flocks separated. How they did it I could not understand, but their manner was harsh and strin- gent. Nor were these watchful guardians dogs; they were bears and wolves who silently darted fierce glances at one another. They seemed more intent on

closely eying one another than on keeping the bleat-
ing lambs in line.

I asked the shepherds why those wolves and bears
worked so hard in the midst of so quiet and docile a
flock, and why there were two flocks although the
sheep were all alike. An old man, stripping the wool
from one of the sheep, showed me a brand mark and
explained that that was the symbol of one flock. Then
he did the same with an animal from the other flock,
explaining that the two different brands meant two
different ownerships. But, although I scrutinized the
marks closely, I found it impossible to distinguish the
two brands. They were identical. So were those on
all the other sheep I examined, one by one. This
mark had something ominous and repugnant about it,
but I couldn't remember what it stood for. I called the
shepherds' attention to the fact that the two brands
were alike, and insisted on knowing why the flocks
were divided. They answered me, with an air of
cunning, that the soil was different. But I showed
them that the grass was everywhere alike. Then they
told me that the flocks had to be divided because
there were too many sheep, and that if they were
placed together they would trample on the wolves and
bears. When I retorted that I couldn't be satisfied
with such a silly and unlikely reason and insisted that

they were trying to fool me, they ended by telling me: "We don't know why. But there are two flocks; that's the Emperor's order."

It was a serene morning. The sheep were silently grazing, the air was full of bucolic peace. The sun was rising behind the mountain ridges, but the valley was so motionless and still that my heart filled with fright. I thought I ought to ask the shepherds some other questions, but they were no longer near me. Then, all of a sudden, their trumpets resounded in the distance like the fierce stamping of horses. — The waitress was knocking at the door, bringing me my breakfast coffee.

It was only a few minutes' ride to Tempelhof Airport through the already crowded streets in the center of Berlin, past tall new buildings of steel and glass, past ruins and jammed sidewalks, in the crisp air of a new day. The field was swarming with travelers. Planes were leaving in every direction— for Hamburg, Düsseldorf, Munich, Frankfurt, and many other points. We were all seated in our plane waiting to take off when a paralyzed old lady was carried in by an American employee of the airline. But no sooner was she settled in her seat after a good deal of effort than it turned out that she was on the wrong plane. So they had to carry her down the plane ramp again like a big parcel. As we veered about, the last houses of Berlin, with their red roofs, rocked beneath us as if in a cradle. The lakes glistened among the trees in the parks; the cars, like rows of ants, moved along the highways. But already clouds and fog shrouded the landscape—and the invisible area of East Germany. We flew in this thick mysterious veil, through some bureaucratic corridor or other, over obscure cities and fields, until we landed beyond the artificial boundaries, on the other side. We were at Frankfurt.

Here I had to change planes and had a two-hour wait before proceeding to Italy. This, I was told, was the busiest airfield in Germany, where all lines crossed. I settled back to wait in the garish modern waiting room. At the bar an elegant German couple who spoke Italian recognized me and introduced themselves. We entered into conversation. They were leaving for Hamburg in half an hour. The woman, tall and still beautiful, was head of a publishing house; her husband was a man of the theater and had translated Pirandello. They told me about a trip they had made to Italy the previous summer. Near Merano they had stopped, without getting out of their car, to ask an old, poorly dressed peasant the name of the bridge over which they were passing. They had addressed him in Italian; he replied as though he had not understood the question, telling them the name of his dog. He answered courteously only when interrogated in German. He gave them all the information they needed, and then asked for a cigarette. They gave him a whole pack. The peasant was so amazed, so flabbergasted at this unexpected gift, that he began to stammer, searching vainly for some expression to convey his thanks adequately. Finally, after much stammering, he suddenly uttered a cry from the heart: *"Heil Hitler!"* It was like a call of salvation, a shout of liberation. The German couple was as astounded as I was that it could have been an Italian.

I remained alone at the windows of the waiting room; there were cameras, perfumes, made-up duty-free parcels, purchasable only with dollars. With the few German marks I had left I could buy only a pen-knife with a picture of Frankfurt showing its bridge and river in color on the mother-of-pearl. This iridescent conventional scene, with its Gothic scroll against the sky, was my last image of Germany. The cars passed over the bridge, the pointed belfries soared skyward, the ships' funnels belched smoke, the green trees were mirrored in the river's intimate flow. I was leaving behind this land which is in the heart of Europe, itself shaped like a heart, and which,

swollen with obscure sentiments concealed beneath
the protective armor of its breast, stubbornly beats to
the rhythms of its machines. It has two ventricles, a
right and a left, which do not alternate and do not
know each other. Its valves are perfect, its heartbeats
regular and sound. Everything is in place; everything
has been miraculously restored. Factories and
cathedrals, refugee camps and crystal palaces, super-
highways, lights, riches, dark forests and placid
countrysides, glittering power and monotonous dili-
gence, secretive intimacy and fashionable luxury, history and mythology and work—all are shut up in this
heart.

Yet I felt there was something missing. Or rather
that something was hiding there; or that something
was split, divided, removed, devastated. I felt there
was a dark silence beneath the regular, mechanical
beating of that great organ, a hollow silence made
up of questions and terror. That heart, that mighty
heart, that mysterious heart, was an empty heart.

But the engines were roaring. We had climbed above
the clouds and were cruising between two strata. The
one below was snowy and light, with just a hint of
bright transparencies; the one above was very high.

Flying very fast, we were now over the Alps. In the cloud openings to our left we could see, in a double image, the vaguely glittering rainbow of two yellow-and-black spirals: Lake Constance and the Rhine. In front of us, colorless and covered with dull patches of fog, the Lake of Zurich marked the boundary of the rolling plain of Germany. Then suddenly the white mountain peaks loomed. Here we were immersed in clouds and gray mist, flying over the faintly whitening shadow of the city of Zurich and the ghostlike walls of snow. Then all at once the sky on high became radiantly blue. A marvelous dome of azure light overhung the swollen expanse of cumulus clouds covering the earth. We danced in the wind. The plane was battered by violent forces that pulled and shook it. The clouds gleamed in the sunlight beneath a pure sky, with blue islands on the horizon that resembled an aerial sea.

And now we had really come to the sea. I recognized its shape, the curve of the coastline. It was the whole of Liguria, from Portofino to La Spezia, dark, rocky, high above the sea, ridged and youthful as it extended and protruded toward the ever winding shore against which the waves were beating. Elba was buffeted by the stiff wind that agitated the Tyrrhenian Sea and drove the clouds like panic-stricken

flocks into the valleys. Then, white and blue and sunlight. In sky-blue clarity we flew toward the coast with
its double edges of foam, green and rose-colored in
the sun. We flew over a wavelike series of promon-
tories, over the bow-shaped Maremma, in a sky that
farther south, toward Rome, darkened with storm. To
the right the sun sank—orange, yellow, purple, di-
aphanous, brilliantly ablaze—among distant layers of
clouds on the horizon, green reflections of the sea,
unexpected cold flames, and red shooting stars. But
now the sunset was behind us; we were flying toward
the dark Italian South.

A NOTE ON THE TYPE

THIS BOOK was set on the Linotype in BODONI
BOOK, a printing type so called after Giambat-
tista Bodoni (1740–1813), a celebrated printer
and type designer of Rome and Parma. Bodoni
Book as produced by the Linotype company is
not a copy of any one of Bodoni's fonts, but is a
composite, modern version of the Bodoni manner.
Bodoni's innovations in printing-type style were a
greater degree of contrast in the "thick and thin"
elements of the letters and a sharper and more
angular finish of details.

Composed, printed, and bound by
Kingsport Press, Inc., Kingsport, Tennessee.
Paper manufactured by
S. D. Warren Co., Boston
Typography and binding design by
VINCENT TORRE

A NOTE ABOUT THE AUTHOR

CARLO LEVI was born in Turin, Italy, on November 29, 1902, and early in life abandoned music for painting. An active anti-Fascist, he was arrested twice during 1934–5, and imprisoned for a year in Lucania; he then lived in France until 1942, but after his return to Florence was arrested once more, in 1943. After 1945 he became internationally known as a writer with the publication of *Christ Stopped at Eboli,* which was translated into twenty languages and was widely read throughout the world after the war. In 1946 *Paura della Libertà* appeared, a book of reflections on the crisis of civilization which Carlo Levi had written in France seven years before and which was published later in the United States under the title *Of Fear and Freedom.* In 1950 *L'Orologio* (*The Watch*) was published, a novel which, in the resurgence of Italy in 1945, represented a sequel to *Christ Stopped at Eboli.* Since 1956 Levi has written three books as a result of his encounters with three very different civilizations: *Le Parole Sono Pietre,* telling of his days in Sicily, which won the Premio Viareggio in 1956 and was published in 1958 here as *Words Are Stones; Il Futuro Ha un Cuore Antico,* the story of a "sentimental journey" through Russia; and the present travel narrative about Germany.

January 1962